In [illegible] he

Bible's Inspiration

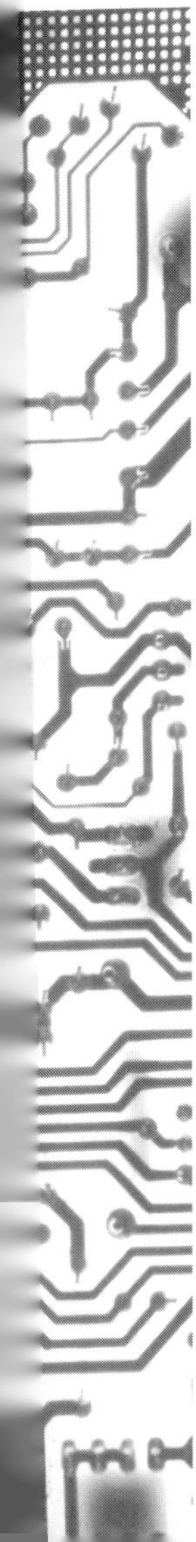

Bert Thompson, Ph.D.

APOLOGETICS PRESS

Apologetics Press, Inc.
230 Landmark Drive
Montgomery, Alabama 36117-2752

(Third Edition)
ISBN: 0-932859-60-7

TABLE OF CONTENTS

DEDICATION

This volume is dedicated to Don Deffenbaugh and Bobby Key, whose love for God's Word has been unwavering, whose defense of the Truth has been balanced, and whose knowledge of the Bible has been a blessing to the lives of untold thousands.

IN DEFENSE OF THE BIBLE'S INSPIRATION

Knowledge and truth are precious commodities. As a body of factual information and legitimate principles, knowledge is indispensable in human relationships. Truth, as knowledge justifiably believed, represents a fundamental reality that transcends both the provincial and the temporal. Most people are desirous of obtaining a certain amount of knowledge that they then can put to good use in their everyday lives. And, undoubtedly, most people prefer not be deceived, but instead prefer to be dealt with honestly and truthfully. One of the Ten Commandments, in fact, was based upon just such a concept: "Thou shalt not bear false witness against thy neighbor" (Exodus 20:16).

Truthfulness always has been the basis for the moral, legal, and ethical codes of nations. And, an abiding respect for truth has undergirded the legitimacy of those codes. "Buy the truth, and sell it not," said the Proverbs writer (23:23). He who possesses correct knowledge has within him the potential to discern, and then act upon, truth. Knowledge frees from the shackles of ignorance; truth frees from the shackles of error. Indeed, knowledge and truth **are** precious commodities.

While almost anyone you ask will admit, **in theory**, that knowledge and truth are indispensable attributes of a sensible, everyday existence, **in practice** many people live out that daily existence as if knowledge and truth ultimately do not matter. Much of mankind lives according to an abstract, confusing, and largely inconsistent system of personal behavior. This is a bit odd, to say the least. In most matters, a man likely will insist upon complete **objectivity**. For example, in regard to his eating habits he might say, "I will not eat this food; it contains bacterial toxins that will kill me." In regard to matters of civil law, he might suggest, "That action is illegal; it violates my rights."

Yet when it comes to religion in general, and Christianity in particular, **subjectivity** rules the day. People can be so certain about their beliefs in the physical realm, but so nebulous about their beliefs in the spiritual realm. For example, on occasion when a person who believes in God is asked if God does, in fact, exist, he may opine: "I **believe** He exists," or "I **hope** He exists," or "I **think** He exists." But rarely do you hear him say boldly, "I **know** He exists." Or, if a Christian is asked the question, "Do you **know** you are saved?," the response may go something like this: "I believe that I am," or "I hope that I am," or "I think that I am." But all too rarely do you hear someone confidently assert, "Yes, I **know** that I am saved."

This is indeed a sad state of affairs. We now have progressed to the point where, in matters as mundane as food choices or legal wrangling, objectivity is an absolute requirement. Meanwhile, in the much more important area of spiritual matters, we not only expect, but in many cases insist upon, a subjectivity that we would not tolerate in any other sphere of our lives. It is as if the pluralistic postmodernism that has affected secular society (the "I'm OK, you're OK"/"Who am I to judge?" concept) finally has made its way into the spiritual community as well. Apparently, some among us either once knew but long since have forgotten, or never understood in the first place, the proper concept of truth. Similarly, we either have forgotten, or no longer care, about the damage that an improper concept of truth can cause.

The time has come for Christians to embolden themselves once again with the same high regard for truth that Jesus expressed when He stated: "And ye shall know the truth, and the truth shall make you free" (John 8:32). Christianity is not an "I-hope-so/pie-in-the-sky-by-and-by" kind of religion based upon some esoteric, fairy-tale-like concept. Rather, it is rooted and grounded in the provable existence of the one true God, and the verifiable nature of the historical facts surrounding the life, death, and resurrection of His Son. When the apostle John wrote to comfort and reassure first-century Christians who found themselves in the midst of numerous trials and persecutions, he said: "These things have I written unto you, that ye may **know** that ye have eternal life, even unto you that believe on the name of the Son of God" (1 John 5:13, emp. added). Thus, according to both Jesus and John, a person not only can know something, but he can know that he knows it.

There are certain undeniable, critically important implications standing behind this kind of firm and confident declaration. Consider the following. If a person cannot **know** (with certainty) that God exists, then he cannot know (with certainty) that the Bible is His inspired Word. If a person cannot know that the Bible is the inspired Word of God, then he cannot know that Jesus is God's Son, for the Bible provides the evidentiary basis for such a claim. If a person cannot know that Christ is God's Son, then he cannot know that he is saved. Yet John specifically stated: "These things have I written unto you, that ye may **know** that ye have eternal life...."

The simple fact is–Christians are not agnostics! The agnostic suggests, "I **cannot know** whether God exists." Christians, on the other hand, **know** that God exists (cf. Psalm 46:10). Consider the alternative. Do Christians serve a God Who "may" or "may not" exist? Do Christians believe, and ask others to believe, the testimony of a Bible that "may" or "may not" be inspired? Do Christians trust, obey, and place their faith in a Christ Who "may" or "may not" be the Son of God? Hardly!

Even the casual reader will discern the close relationship among these vital issues. Knowledge of God's existence is foundational, which is why I have marshaled the evidence for it (Thompson, 2000, pp. 123-181). Knowledge of Christ's Sonship is pivotal, which is why I have documented the facts that attend it (Thompson, 1999, pp. 19-32). Knowledge of salvation is essential, which is why I have assembled the testimony from Scripture that attests to it (Thompson, 1998a; 1998b). But no less important is the evidence that establishes the inspiration of God's Word–the topic to which I now direct your attention.

THE NEED FOR REVELATION FROM GOD

With the existence of God established, it becomes reasonable to think that such a Creator-God would wish to communicate with His creation. Mankind shows evidence of high intelligence, kindness, goodness, justice, and many other unique characteristics. Since it is inconceivable that the Creator could be inferior to His creation in any fashion, and since the effect never is greater than the cause, it is inevitable that God would exhibit infinite intelligence, kindness, goodness, justice, etc. Therefore, some form of personal communication between the intelligent Creator and His intelligent creature would be expected. Else, how could mankind ever come to know, or appreciate, certain aspects of the Creator, or understand what the Creator might possibly require of the beings He had created? Furthermore, some form of revelation from the Creator would be essential in order to instruct mankind in certain areas, such as the following.

The Character of God. While something of God's essence, power, and wisdom can be gleaned vaguely from the vastness and marvelous intricacies of the creation itself, a more concrete communication is needed to establish the exact nature of His character.

The Origin of Evil. As mankind found itself adrift in a sea of evil, pain, and suffering, the question eventually would arise: Why? Man thus needed to be educated concerning the exact reason(s) for his predicament.

Mankind's Origin. Without revelation to the contrary, men might come to the conclusion that they owe their ultimate origin to "accidental forces of nature," rather than to the omnipotence of a divine Creator. The confusion of modern-day evolutionary theories is evidence aplenty of this.

Mankind's Purpose. Man–left to his own devices–never could understand completely the ultimate purpose for his creation at the hand of an Almighty God. With no adequately defined role, and no immediate or future goals, he would wander aimlessly, from cradle to grave, in a sea of uncertainty.

Mankind's Destiny. In the absence of divine revelation, man never would know with certainty anything about the existence of life beyond this one. He therefore might conclude incorrectly–as many have in every generation–that this life is all there is. The urgency of mankind having access to this knowledge is evinced by the general despair of those who reject the concept of supernatural revelation.

A revelation from God might take almost any form. God could choose to communicate with His creation directly via word of mouth, through messengers (e.g., angels), or through dreams and visions. For that matter, He could choose any means that suited the occasion. Seemingly, however, the most appropriate medium for long-term results would be one that ensured permanence. That is to say, it would withstand the test of time, and could be passed faithfully from generation to generation throughout human history. One possible way to accomplish such a goal would be to produce the revelation in a written form that could be duplicated and distributed as needed, thus benefitting the whole of mankind across the ages.

The question then becomes: Is there any evidence that mankind possesses such a revelation? And the answer to that question is: Yes, evidence does exist to establish the claim that God has given mankind His revelation in the written form known as the Bible. B.C. Goodpasture, the distinguished editor of the *Gospel Advocate* for almost forty years, wrote:

> The nature and contents of the Bible are such that the rank and file of its readers in all generations have recognized God as its author. Man would not have written such a book, if he could; and could not, if he would. It moves on a superhuman plane in design, in nature, and in teaching. It caters not to worldly desire and ambition. It condemns much which men in the flesh highly prize, and commends much which they despise. Its thoughts are not the thoughts of men (1970, p. 54).

Harold Lindsell, former editor of *Christianity Today*, remarked:

> Had God chosen not to reveal Himself, man could never have known Him. And man can never know more about God than God chooses to disclose.... Whatever knowledge of God is available exists solely because God has chosen to make it known. This is His self-revelation (1976, p. 28).

God's written revelation makes it clear that in the past He provided that "self-revelation" in a variety of ways. The Maker of the Universe manifested His presence in the works of His creative genius (Psalm 19:1; Romans 1:20-21). He spoke to various men and women in a direct, word-of-mouth fashion (Genesis 3:9-16; Numbers 12:8). He revealed Himself through visions and dreams (Genesis 20:3; Numbers 12:6; Isaiah 29: 10-11; Ezekiel 1:3-4; Daniel 2:19; Amos 1:1). He addressed His creation through angels (Genesis 16:10-12; 18:13-14; 22: 11ff.; 32:1-2; Acts 7:38). On unique occasions, He even made known His presence through such media as "a still, small voice" (1 Kings 19:12), the mouth of a donkey (Numbers

22:28), and a bright cloud (Matthew 17:5). God's greatest revelation of Himself, however, was in the person of His Son, Jesus Christ (John 3:16; 14:9; Colossians 2:9).

Lacking adequate revelation from God, we would have no accurate way of understanding what we needed to know regarding God, His Son, our place in the Creation, and many other topics of ultimate importance to humanity. We would have no objective standard upon which to base ethics and morals. We would know little of the ministry and message of Jesus of Nazareth. We would have no information regarding the theological purpose of His crucifixion and resurrection —namely, that they were essential ingredients in God's plan to offer ruined man a way of escape from the devastating consequences of his sin (Matthew 20:28; 26:28). We would know nothing of how to enter that sacred body of saved souls, the church (Ephesians 5:23; 1 Corinthians 12:13), or how, once we had entered, to worship God correctly. Without God's revelation, we would know utterly nothing about these important spiritual matters that impact our eternal destiny. Perhaps it was with such things in mind that Arthur W. Pink wrote these beautiful words:

> If it were announced upon reliable authority that on a certain date in the near future an angel from heaven would visit New York and would deliver a sermon upon the invisible world, the future destiny of man, or the secret deliverance from the power of sin, what an audience he would command! There is no building in that city large enough to accommodate the crowd which would throng to hear him. If upon the next day, the newspapers were to give a verbatim report of his discourse, how eagerly it would be read! And yet, we have between the covers of the Bible not merely an angelic communication, but a Divine revelation. How great then is our wickedness if we undervalue and despise it! And yet we do (1976, p. 103).

Truly, we should be grateful to God for providing us with a revelation that could be retained in a permanent form, studied faithfully, and used profitably by all of mankind.

WHAT DOES THE BIBLE CONTAIN?

The fact that the Bible exists in the first place brings to mind the question: What does the Bible contain? It contains two things: (1) known facts; and (2) revelation. What is the difference between the two?

When we say that the Bible contains "known facts," we mean that it contains information known to the people of that time and place. For example, if the Bible mentions people known as Hittites (Exodus 23:28), then historical records could verify their existence. If the Bible mentions that the Roman emperor Caesar Augustus commanded that a census be taken at a certain time (Luke 2:1), then we could corroborate the truthfulness of such a statement.

But to say that the Bible "contains" known facts, implies that it also contains something else. That "something else" is revelation. By definition, revelation designates the unveiling of facts and truths to man by God–facts and truths that man, on his own, otherwise could not have known. Revelation has reference to the communication of information.

Compare and contrast the following. When Moses wrote in the book of Numbers about Israel's wilderness wanderings, he did not need revelation from God to do so. He was their leader during that period, and simply wrote what he observed as an eyewitness. When Luke penned the book in the New Testament that bears his name, he did not need revelation from God to do so. He acknowledged as much when he said: "It seemed good to me also, **having traced the course of all things accurately from the first**, to write unto thee in order, most excellent Theophilus" (Luke 1:3, emp. added).

Luke had been on certain of the missionary journeys, and thus was able to write from firsthand experience.

On the other hand, notice Moses' statement in Deuteronomy 29:29: "The secret things belong unto Jehovah our God; but **the things that are revealed** belong unto us and to our children forever, that we may do all the words of this law" (emp. added). As an illustration of this fact, we may observe that Moses would have had absolutely no way to know the details of the Creation week (Genesis 1:1ff.), unless God Himself had revealed those details to him. Nor could the apostle John have described in such a beautiful panorama the splendors of heaven (as he did within the book of Revelation), unless God first described to John the splendors of heaven.

On occasion, the various Bible writers could, and did, place in print what they saw, or what they had been told by credible witnesses. When they penned such matters, they had no need of revelation from God, since they wrote from firsthand experience. At times, however, they wrote about things they neither had experienced nor had been told by others. When they did so, it was God's revelation that provided them the information they needed (Amos 3:7; Daniel 2:28; Ephesians 3:3-5).

THE TWO TYPES OF REVELATION

There are two different types of revelation. **General** (or natural) revelation designates the revelation that God has provided of Himself in nature (cf. Romans 1:20-21, Acts 14:17, Psalm 19:1, et al.). **Special** (or supernatural) revelation is the name that designates the revelation that God has provided within the Bible.

General Revelation

General revelation comes to man through nature. The first six verses of Psalm 19 declare that God has given a revelation of Himself in nature that constantly testifies of the Creator. In Romans 1:20, Paul stated that "the invisible things of him since the creation of the world are clearly seen, being perceived **through the things that are made**, even his everlasting power and divinity; that they may be without excuse" (emp. added).

The Scriptures teach that general revelation is universal. At no time in history has God left Himself without a witness of Himself (Acts 14:17). General revelation is universal in both scope and territory. God's glory can be seen whenever and wherever a heavenly body is observed. It can be seen in the glistening of a gorgeous afternoon rainbow, or in the still, sweet waters of a gently flowing brook through a rainforest. Though men often refuse to recognize and accept God's revelation of Himself in nature, it abides nevertheless.

Just as general revelation was present before man sinned in the Garden of Eden, so it is present after his fall. But general revelation is not always understood as it should be, because man's mind has become corrupt. The reason for man's apostasy and mental depravity is due to his initial fall from Heaven's favor (Genesis 3). Man was created in the image of God, yet became a rebel who was subject to evil passions and subsequently blinded to the spiritual values that are so important (2 Corinthians 4:3-4). His heart also became subject to corruption (Romans 3:10-18; Ephesians 2:1ff.).

With the fall of man, not an **evolution** but a **devolution** began. As a result of his disobedience to God's laws, man has become afflicted with a blindness that sometimes prevents him from understanding God's revelation in nature. The noetic effects of sin have darkened his mind so that he often does not grasp the message of the revelation of God that appears all around him on a daily basis.

As great as general revelation is, however, it is deficient in and of itself. For many, nature has ceased to be a perspicuous revelation of God. It may have been so before sin entered the world, but even if it were, man's nature now has become so polluted that he steadfastly refuses to read the divine script around him. General revelation simply is not enough. It never was intended to be. It does not afford man the reliable knowledge of God and other important spiritual matters that he needs for salvation. It therefore is inadequate (by itself) as the sole foundation of a person's faith. From nature alone, man never would be able to infer the need for a personal Savior. Therefore, God has seen fit to give man a second type of revelation.

Special Revelation

God has revealed Himself in the sixty-six books of the Bible in a most specific fashion. Speaking in general terms, there has been only one permanent supernatural revelation, i.e., the supernatural revelation found in the Scriptures. Actually, however, God has disclosed Himself throughout human history in at least three different ways: theophanies, direct communications, and miracles.

Theophanies are appearances of God Himself. He is spoken of as dwelling between the cherubim (Psalm 80:1; 99:1). He appeared in fire, clouds, and smoke (cf. Genesis 15:17, Exodus 3:2, 19:9, 16ff., 33:9, and Psalm 78:14; 99:7). He appeared in stormy winds (Job 38:1; 40:6; Psalm 18:10-16). Theophany reached its highest point during the incarnation, in which Jesus Christ became flesh and dwelt among men (Colossians 1:19; 2:9).

God disclosed Himself in a second way through **direct communications**. In doing so, He made His thoughts and will known to men. Sometimes it was through an audible voice (Genesis 2:16; 3:8-19; 4:6-15; 9:1,8,12; 32:26; Exodus 19:9; Deuteronomy 5:4-5; 1 Samuel 3:4). He worked through dreams (Numbers 12:6; Deuteronomy 13:1-6; 1 Samuel 28:6; Joel 2:28). He communicated through visions (Isaiah 6; 21: 6ff.; Ezekiel 1-3; 8-11; Daniel 1:17; 2:19; 7-10). And lastly,

God has communicated His thoughts and will to men via the Holy Spirit (Mark 13:11; Luke 12:12; John 14:17; 15:26; 16:13; 20:22; Acts 6:10; 8:29; 2 Peter 1:20-21).

God also chose to reveal Himself through **miracles** that not only showcased His power and presence, but also emphasized great truths as well. They confirmed the words of prophecy, and stood as evidence of God's omnipotence among the people that He had created. The greatest of these miracles was the incarnation.

Revelation is of word and fact; as such, it is historical in nature. Its purposes are many, but among those purposes are redemption and salvation. God's revelation was progressive and unfolding in character–dim at first, then gradually increasing in light until its fullness finally arrived. As Harold Lindsell observed:

> This revelation of God of which I have been speaking has become inscripturated. It has come down to us in written form. Thus, there are two Words: the Word of God incarnate, Jesus Christ, and the Word of God written, the Bible. It is the Word of God written that reveals the Word of God incarnate to man. The Bible, then, is **the** Word of God and it is of this Word we now speak. When we say the Bible is the Word of God, it makes no difference whether the writers of Scripture gained their information by direct revelation from God as in the case of the Book of Revelation, or whether they researched matters as Luke did, or whether they got their knowledge from extant sources, court records, or even by word of mouth. The question we must now ask is whether what they wrote, wherever they may have secured their knowledge, can be trusted. This brings us to the doctrine of inspiration, which is clearly taught in the Bible itself (1976, p. 30).

THE BIBLE'S CLAIMS FOR ITS OWN INSPIRATION

Imagine, if you can, that somehow you could have access to every religious book that has ever been written. Imagine, also, that you could run those books through some sort of a sieve, to winnow out only those volumes that claimed to be a creed book, by which you should pattern and live your life. That, admittedly, would be a tough test and one that, likely, very few books could pass. Then, imagine further that you could take the books that passed this test, and run them through a second sieve. This time you would winnow out only those books that claimed to be both a creed book for regulating your life **and inspired of God**. Interestingly, you could count that number on the fingers of two hands.

The claim of inspiration at the hand of God is rare indeed. Sadly, misguided devotees of various religions clamor about, defending this book or that book as allegedly being "inspired of God," when, in fact, the books themselves do not even make such a claim. So, the first question that should be asked of any volume for which inspiration is touted is this: Does the **book itself** claim to be inspired?

When it comes to the Bible, that question can be answered in the affirmative. In his first letter to his coworker, Timothy, Paul stated: "All scripture is given by inspiration of God, and is profitable for doctrine, for reproof, for correction, for instruction in righteousness: that the man of God may be perfect, throughly furnished unto all good works" (2 Timothy 3:16-17). Peter wrote: "Knowing this first, that no prophecy of scripture is of private interpretation. For no prophecy ever came by the will of man: but men spake from God, being moved by the Holy Spirit" (2 Peter 1:20-21). When he wrote his first epistle to the Christians at Corinth, Paul reminded them:

> But we received, not the spirit of the world, but the spirit which is from God; that we might know the things that were freely given to us of God. Which things also we speak, not in words which man's wisdom teacheth, but which the Spirit teacheth; combining spiritual things with spiritual words (1 Corinthians 2:12-13).

Furthermore, statements such as "God said…" or "these are the words of the Lord…" appear thousands of times in both the Old and New Testaments. Moses wrote in Exodus 20:1: "And God spake all these words...." The psalmist wrote in 119:89: "For ever, O Jehovah, Thy word is settled in heaven." In Matthew 22:31, the Lord asked: "Have ye not read that which was spoken unto you by God?" In fact, "[t]here are 2,700 such statements in the Old Testament alone, all of which make direct claim that the Bible is the Word of God" (Ridenour, 1967, p. 2).

When the Bible claims to be "inspired," what is meant by that term? The English term "inspiration" derives from the Latin *inspirare*, which means "to breathe upon or into something." The five English words, "given by inspiration of God," in the King James Version of 1611 actually are translated from the single Greek adjective, *theopneustos*, which is derived from two Greek root words (*theos*–God, *pneo*–to blow or breathe). *Pneuma*, meaning "spirit," comes from the verb *pneo. Pneustos*, then, might mean "spirited," and *theopneustos* would mean God-spirited, God-breathed, filled with the breath of God, the product of the divine breath (or Spirit), or given by God through the Spirit. The word implies an influence from without, producing effects that are beyond natural powers. "The book that is in this sense inspired is one into which something of another spirit or mind has been breathed; in other words, its author has been overshadowed by a power **outside** himself" (Goodpasture, 1970, p. 57, emp. in orig.). In his book, *The Battle for the Bible*, Lindsell stated:

Inspiration may be defined as the inward work of the Holy Spirit in the hearts and minds of chosen men who then wrote the Scriptures so that God got written what He wanted. The Bible in all of its parts constitutes the written Word of God to man. This Word is free from all error in the original autographs. It is wholly trustworthy in matters of history and doctrine. However limited may have been their knowledge, and however much they may have erred when they were not writing sacred Scripture, the authors of Scripture, under the guidance of the Holy Spirit, were preserved from making factual, historical, scientific, or other errors. The Bible does not purport to be a textbook of history, science, or mathematics; yet when the writers of Scripture spoke of matters embraced in these disciples, they did not indite error; they wrote what was true.

The very nature of inspiration renders the Bible infallible, which means that it cannot deceive us. It is inerrant in that it is not false, mistaken, or defective. Inspiration extends to all parts or the written Word of God and it includes the guiding hand of the Holy Spirit even in the selection of the words of Scripture.

Inspiration involved infallibility from start to finish. God the Holy Spirit by nature cannot lie or be the author of untruth. If the Scripture is inspired at all, it must be infallible. If any part of it is not infallible, then that part cannot be inspired. If inspiration allows for the possibility of error then inspiration ceases to be inspiration (1976, pp. 30-31).

Theologically, then, "inspiration" is used for the condition of **being directly under divine influence**. Paul's point was that every scripture is "God breathed." [The word "scripture" in 2 Timothy 3:16 refers primarily to the Old Testament Scriptures. However, as the New Testament was written, it, too, was referred to as "scripture." Peter, for example, referred to Paul's epistles as authoritative "scripture" (2 Peter 3:15-16). Thus, the phrase "all scripture" refers to both testaments.]

One searches in vain in the Bible for an exact statement containing the details of **how** God related to the apostles and others in the production of the words they spoke or wrote. We know that the Spirit spoke by men and that His word was on their tongues (2 Samuel 23:2). We know that the Holy Spirit spoke by the mouth of men (Acts 1:16). We know that the things spoken were in words taught by the Holy Spirit (1 Corinthians 2:12-13). But no one knows the exact details of how the Spirit guided, superintended, guaranteed, and produced the end result. There are hidden details here that we may not presume to know. Holy men of God spoke as they were moved by the Spirit (2 Peter 1:20-21), guaranteeing that all Scripture is inspired of God (2 Timothy 3:16-17). But one must be content with these and similar statements. God simply has not spelled out the details of how His Spirit entered into the minds of the writers, or how He worked with their hands as they wrote. The point is that the work produced was God's Word, not man's. As such it bears His divine stamp.

When Peter wrote in 2 Peter 1:20-21 that "men spake from God, being **moved** by the Holy Spirit," he employed the Greek word *pheromenoi*, which literally means "borne along." His point was that the Bible writers did not speak from themselves, but instead were "borne along" by God's Holy Spirit to write what they did. The Bible writers never credited their words to mere human reason. Both Old and New Testament passages bear this out. In 2 Samuel 23:2, it is written: "The Spirit of Jehovah spake by me, And his word was upon my tongue." In Acts 1:16, Luke observed that "the Holy Spirit spake before by the mouth of David...." Likely, however, the best explanatory passage regarding inspiration would be Paul's commentary in 1 Corinthians 2:12-13, where he affirmed that the information the Bible writers received came not from human wisdom, but rather directly from God. Further, that wisdom was not expressed in man's choice of words, but via words guided by the Holy Spirit.

There are several different ideas concerning the inspiration of the Bible. "Perhaps it would be more accurate to say that different men believe in different levels of inspiration" (Baxter, 1971, p. 171). Let us now turn our attention to some of the various theories of inspiration.

Universal (Naturalistic) Inspiration. This theory holds that the Bible is inspired only in the sense that writers and artists are "inspired" when they produce great works of literature, music, or art. Actually this is the theory that certain men are inspired in the sense that they are exceptionally talented. In this sense, Shakespeare, Milton, Beethoven, Browning, Frost, and Van Gogh all were "inspired." This theory of inspiration holds that, in essence, the Bible is just like any other book. Although God may have given the authors an unusual ability to convey thoughts, the Bible is, after all, a human production without supernatural guidance. But, of course, this is not really inspiration at all. It might be called "natural genius," but not inspiration. As Wayne Jackson pointed out in his text, *Fortify Your Faith*:

> This theory is to be rejected for the following reasons. (a) It makes liars out of the N.T. writers who claimed the Holy Spirit as the source of their works. (b) The biblical documents are vastly superior to the ablest production of men. (c) It leaves the marvelous unity of the Bible as an inexplicable mystery. (d) If the Scriptures were the result of natural genius, modern genius could make them obsolete; instead, the Bible remains the world's best-seller (1974, p. 52).

Thought (Dynamic or Concept) Inspiration. This view asserts that the "thoughts" of the men are inspired, but not the words. According to this idea, the important thing is that great spiritual truths be conveyed to the reader; it really does not matter what words are used, or even whether the words described events that actually occurred. This theory may sound spiritual and pious, but it has grave problems. The human authors may have understood only partially what God was revealing to them, and in restating it in their own words, they may have interjected considerable error. It is possible to convey precise thoughts and ideas only by using precise words! If the words are unimportant, then the thoughts, which come from the words, are entirely subjective. In other words:

> But what good are "infallible ideas" if channeled through "fallible" words? The truth is, one can no more have ideas without words than he can have a tune without notes or a sum without figures. The very idea is absurd! And I tell you honestly, it never ceases to puzzle me how some modernists can do such marvelous "word studies" from the text of the Bible, at the same time denying the "verbal" inspiration thereof. If the words of the sacred volume are uninspired, why the interest in them? Do scholars produce volumes of "word studies" on Shakespeare? (Jackson, 1974, p. 52).

Neo-Orthodox Inspiration. During the twentieth century, another view of inspiration was advanced by men like Karl Barth. L.S. Chafer, in his book, *Major Bible Themes*, explained.

> While not necessarily denying that supernatural elements exist in the writing of Scripture, this view acknowledges that there are errors in the Bible and thus the Bible cannot be taken literally as true. Neo-orthodoxy holds that God speaks through the Scriptures and uses them as a means by which to communicate truth to us. Accordingly, the Bible becomes a channel of divine revelation much as a beautiful flower or a lovely sunset communicates the concept that God is the Creator. The Bible under this theory be-

> comes true only as it is comprehended and truth is realized by the individual reader. The history of this view demonstrates that no two of its advocates exactly agree as to what the Bible actually teaches, and like the view of partial inspiration, leaves the individual as the final authority concerning what is true and what is false (1926, p. 19).

Speaking in support of this theory, Emil Brunner once said that those "conservatives" who consider the Bible objectively and propositionally to be the Word of God are setting up a "paper pope" and thereby commit "bibliolatry" (see Merideth, 1972, pp. 377-378). Such an erroneous view of inspiration obviously contradicts the Bible's claims for its own inspiration, and leaves people with little more than ethical subjectivism as their standard.

Encounter Inspiration. This theory holds that the Bible is a **vehicle** of revelation but **is not itself** a divine revelation. It becomes "inspired" when, and only when, it "inspires" the reader. It may well be the medium through which a person encounters God in an act of faith, but it is a human document nevertheless, and as such it is subject to human error throughout. According to this particular theory, then, inspiration becomes entirely subjective. One must have as much faith in his "encounter" session as the Christian has in Scripture. A passage that may be "inspired" to one reader may be utterly "uninspired" to someone else who reads the very same passage. Scripture therefore loses all of its evangelistic power.

Dictation (Mechanical) Inspiration. Some Bible critics claim that God dictated the Scriptures (every word, every punctuation mark, etc.) to men who were little more than mechanical stenographers who dutifully copied it all down. If God dictated the Bible, however, the style of writing and the vocabulary of the Bible would be the same throughout. Yet a simple reading of the Scriptures proves that the mechanical dictation viewpoint is without basis in fact. The personality and style of each author are evident in every book of the Bible. In many instances, the writers displayed their own fears and feelings, expressed their private prayers for God's deliverance, or in a host of other ways interjected their own personalities into the Divine Record. God allowed each man his own individuality and creativity, but worked through them all to inspire His Word. While inspiration extends to every word of Scripture, it does not rule out human personality and human personal interest. Direct dictation was not God's plan for inspiration.

Verbal, Plenary Inspiration. This is the correct view of inspiration. It holds that men wrote exactly what God wanted them to write, without errors or mistakes, yet with their own personalities in evidence in their writings. By "verbal," we mean that every word in the Bible is there because God permitted it by the direction of the Holy Spirit. By "plenary" (from the Latin, *plenus*–full), we mean that **every part** of the Bible is inspired, with nothing having been omitted.

In other words, by employing what we today call verbal (word-for-word), plenary (full) inspiration, God ensured that the writings were correct and consistent with His will. This view holds that men wrote exactly what God wanted them to write, without errors or mistakes, yet with their own individual characteristics in evidence. While the various books of the Bible reflect the writers' personalities as expressed in the human element that often is quite evident (type of language used, fears expressed, prayers offered, etc.), it was only by verbal, plenary inspiration that God could convey–objectively and accurately–His Word to mankind.

There is compelling evidence from within the Bible itself about the nature of its inspiration. Immediately after His baptism, Christ went into the wilderness for a crucial confrontation with Satan. When the devil suggested that He convert stones into bread to stay His hunger after a lengthy fast, the Savior replied by quoting Deuteronomy 8:3: "It is written, 'Man shall not live by bread alone, but by every word that proceedeth out of the mouth of God' " (Matthew 4:4). Twice more He stopped the devil's mouth with "It is written...," citing Deuteronomy 6:13,16. In declaring, "It is written," Jesus employed the Greek perfect tense, denoting completed action with abiding results. He thus declared that God's words were written–and remain so.

Jesus endorsed the whole Old Testament at least a dozen times, using such designations as: the Scriptures (John 5:39); the law (John 10:34); the law and the prophets (Matthew 5:17); the law, the prophets, and the psalms (Luke 24:44); or Moses and the prophets (Luke 16:29). In addition, the Son of God quoted, cited from, or alluded to incidents in at least eighteen different Old Testament books. But to what degree did Christ believe in inspiration? The following references document beyond doubt that the Lord affirmed **verbal, plenary** inspiration: In Matthew 5:17-18, Christ exclaimed:

> Think not that I came to destroy the law and the prophets: I came not to destroy, but to fulfill. For verily I say unto you, Till heaven and earth pass away, one jot or one tittle shall in no wise pass from the law, till all things be accomplished.

The "jot" was the smallest Hebrew letter, and the "tittle" was the tiny projection on certain Hebrew letters. When He employed these specific terms as examples, the Lord affirmed the minutest accuracy for the whole of the Old Testament.

In the midst of His discussion with the Sadducees about their denial of the resurrection of the dead (Matthew 22:23-33), Jesus referred to Exodus 3:6 wherein God said to Moses: "I am the God of Abraham, and the God of Isaac, and the God of Jacob." When God spoke these words, Abraham had been dead almost 400 years, yet He still said, "I **am** the God of Abraham." As Jesus correctly pointed out to the Sadducees, "God is not the God of the dead, but of the living" (Matthew 22:32). Thus, Abraham, Isaac, and Jacob must have been living. The only way they could be living was if their spirits continued to survive the death of their bodies. That kind of conscious existence implies a future resurrection of the body–the very point Christ was attempting to make. Of interest is the fact that His entire argument rested on the **tense** of the verb!

In addition to these examples from Christ, there are other clear indications of the recognition of verbal inspiration. David once said: "The Spirit of Jehovah spake by me, and His word was upon my tongue" (2 Samuel 23:2). Observe that the king did not say God's "thoughts" or "concepts" were upon his tongue, but that Jehovah's **word** was upon his tongue. If that is not verbal inspiration, one would be hard pressed to know how verbal inspiration would be expressed.

In the first letter of Paul to the Corinthians, the apostle declared that the things of God were revealed to men by the Spirit. Then, concerning the divine messages, he said, "which things we speak, not in words which man's wisdom teacheth, but which the Spirit teacheth; combining spiritual things with spiritual words" (1 Corinthians 2:13). The words of divine revelation are Spirit-directed words, not words of mere human wisdom. That is **verbal, plenary** inspiration.

The same kind of reliance on a single word was expressed by Paul (as he referred to Genesis 22:18) in Galatians 3:16: "Now to Abraham were the promises spoken, and to his seed. He saith not, 'And to seeds,' as of many; but as of one, 'And to thy **seed**, which is Christ' " (emp. added). The force of his argument rested on the number of the noun (singular, as opposed to plural). In John 8:58, Jesus said: "I say unto you, Before Abraham was born, I **am.**" He was attempting to impress upon the Jews His eternal nature, and to do so, He once again based His entire argument on the tense of the verb.

We should note, however, that this inspiration process applied only to the original autographs of the sacred writings (i.e., the actual document as penned initially by the writer). While the Bible writers were inspired, the scribes, translators, and others who followed were not. This does not mean, as some have suggested, that we do not have God's Word in an accurate form today. The text of the Bible we possess can be trusted and counted as reliable. The modernistic idea which suggests that the copying process through the ages has destroyed the essence of inspiration is a "theological scarecrow to frighten those who are not knowledgeable of the art of transmission of the Bible" (Dickson, 1997, p. 319).

Whenever duplicates of the Scriptures were needed, copies had to be made by hand–a painstaking, time-consuming task requiring extreme concentration and special working conditions. Eventually, an elite group of scribes arose just for this purpose. Geisler and Nix discussed these scribes–the Masoretes–in their book, *A General Introduction to the Bible.*

> The Masoretic period (flourished c. A.D. 500-1000) of Old Testament copying indicates a complete review of established rules, a deep reverence for the Scriptures, and a systematic renovation of transmission techniques.... Copies were made by an official class of sacred scribes who labored under strict rules (1986, pp. 354,467, cf. also pp. 371,374,380).

Anyone who has studied the exacting conditions under which the Masoretes worked, and the lengths to which they went to ensure fidelity in their reproductions, could attest to the fact that their singular goal was accuracy. They were, nevertheless, still human. And humans are prone to mistakes, regardless of the care they take or the strictness of the rules under which they labor. The copyists' task was made all the more difficult by the sheer complexity of the languages involved, and by the various ways in which potential errors could be introduced (even if inadvertently) into the copying process.

Yet, through the centuries, that process was so meticulous, and the number of extant manuscripts available for comparison became so large, that the minute variations that do occur are detected quite easily. Furthermore, these variations are insignificant in nature, and do not affect points of doctrine. Timothy, from his early years, had known the Old Testament "sacred writings" that were able to make him "wise unto salvation" (2 Timothy 3:15). Interestingly, those "sacred writings" were mere copies of the original Old Testament manuscripts, yet had been preserved so faithfully through the years that the apostle Paul could affirm that their original design –to make mankind "wise unto salvation"–remained intact.

Several other points should be clarified as well. First, there is an important difference between revelation and inspiration. Revelation represents the revealing of facts and truths by God to humans. Inspiration is the process by which God guided the writing down of those facts and truths. "Revelation is the body of truth which God desired men to possess; inspiration is the way in which He gave this body of truth to men" (Woods, n.d., p. 6). The whole Bible is the result of inspiration, but not all inspired material was revelatory in nature. Paul could quote pagan poets in Acts 17:28 and Titus 1:12 because he already had access to this information and did not need revelation to employ it. But God inspired him to record these sayings, and to record them accurately. Thus, whether the Bible writer used information already available to him, his own eyewitness accounts, or revelation from God, inspiration guaranteed that it was placed in print in the form that God desired.

Second, uninspired people frequently received revelation in Bible times. The children of Israel, assembled under the burning crags of Sinai, heard God speak in awful majesty (Exodus 20:18-21; Hebrews 12:19), but no one would say that they were inspired. When the martyr Stephen was being stoned, he said: "Behold, I see the heavens opened, and the Son of Man standing on the right hand of God" (Acts 7:56). This was indeed revelation, but not inspiration. Thus, it is correct to say that the Bible **contains** revelation from God, because such a statement implies that it likewise contains items that are not revelatory in nature–which it does (e.g., historical facts already known to the writers). But it is improper to say that the Bible **contains** inspired writings, because such a statement implies that it likewise contains items that are not inspired. Such a position is false, because **all** of the books that comprise the Bible are inspired by the Spirit of God. As Goodpasture rightly remarked: "What he [Paul–BT] said is quite different from the modernistic statement: 'The Bible contains the word of God.' According to Paul, the Bible **is** the word of God; it is all given by inspiration" (1970, p. 55, emp. in orig.).

Revelation assures men that they possess all the information that God decided to make available to them; inspiration certifies that the revelation given to men in written form is truthful and correct. With the death of John, the last New Testament writer, all revelation ceased (simultaneously, inspiration likewise ceased). Since John's death, no new revelation has been given. We have God's word that the Scriptures were "**once for all delivered**" (Jude 3, emp. added).

Third, the fact that a person wrote by inspiration does not mean that he was free from personal sin in his life. Israel's King David penned several Old Testament psalms. The apostle Peter acknowledged that "the Holy Spirit spake before by the mouth of David" (Acts 1:16). Yet this was the very same king who committed adultery with Bathsheba, and had her husband, Uriah the Hittite, slain to cover his sin. Peter himself presented some extremely powerful sermons (e.g., Acts 2:14ff.), and penned two New Testament epistles. Yet he played the hypocrite when he separated himself from the Gentiles to seek favor with the Jews (and received a public rebuke from Paul for it–Galatians 2:11ff.). Thus, while inspiration preserved the integrity of the writer's words as he was "moved by the Holy Spirit," that process neither diminished his freedom of choice nor compelled him to live a sinless life.

Fourth, inspiration was not a twenty-four-hour-a-day process. A few months prior to His death, the Lord informed His disciples that He shortly would enter Jerusalem, where He would suffer and eventually die. Peter, however, rebuked the Lord and said: "Be it far from thee, Lord: this shall never be unto thee" (Matthew 16:22). Obviously, that impetuous utterance was not inspired. In Luke, the story is told of a group of Samaritans who refused aid and comfort to the Lord (9:51ff.). James and John bitterly suggested that the Lord enjoin a "heavenly barbecue" to consume these ill-tempered Samaritans. Their attempt at vengeance–for which they drew the Lord's ire–hardly was inspired. The truth of the matter is that inspiration guided the writers in what they wrote and spoke from God as they were "borne along" by God's Spirit –a process that was not active every minute of every day.

Fifth, inspiration extended to a variety of disparate subjects. Today, it is not uncommon to hear liberal theologians, and those sympathetic with them, suggest that the "spiritual" sections of Scripture are inspired, but that all other portions dealing with matters of history, science, geography, medicine, and the like are not. This concept, known as the doctrine of "partial inspiration," is false. Were it true, everyone who reads the text would have the personal responsibility of wading through the biblical documents to decide which matters are "spiritual" (thus, inspired) and which are not (thus, uninspired). On some occasions, therefore, God would have "breathed" truth, while on others He would have "breathed" error. But the question must be asked: If God cannot handle correctly trivial matters (such as geographical directions, or the name of an individual), why would anyone think that they could trust Him with something as critically important as the safety of their eternal soul and expect Him to handle it in a more appropriate fashion? The psalmist stated: "The **sum** of thy word is truth; And **every one** of thy righteous ordinances endureth for ever" (Psalm 119:160; emp. added). The concept of partial inspiration impugns the integrity and nature of God, conflicts with the evidences for inspiration, and should be rejected.

Sixth, not only did the Bible writers view each others' works as inspired, but no Bible writer ever criticized another. Today, it is not at all unusual for one religious writer to take issue with another, even when they share the same religious views, or are members of the same religious group. But the Bible writers do not fall into that category–even when one might expect them to do so. For example, as mentioned above, Paul rebuked Peter publicly for his dissimulation (Galatians 2:11ff.). Yet Peter never avenged himself by denigrating Paul's writings. In fact, Peter wrote:

> And account that the longsuffering of our Lord is salvation; even as our beloved brother Paul also, according to the wisdom given to him, wrote unto you; as also in all his epistles, speaking in them of these things; wherein are some things hard to be understood, which the ignorant and unstedfast wrest, as they do also the **other scriptures**, unto their own destruction (2 Peter 3:15-16, emp. added).

Note especially that Peter referred to Paul's writings as being classified by the same kind of inspiration as the "other scriptures." Additionally, in defending the right of elders to receive remuneration from the church treasury for their work, Paul quoted Deuteronomy 25:4 and Luke 10:7, classifying them both as "scripture" (1 Timothy 5:18). It is clear that the Bible writers considered each others' works to be inspired–a view we today would do well to entertain.

EVIDENCE OF THE BIBLE'S INSPIRATION

Evidence to substantiate the Bible's claims of its own inspiration can be drawn from two general sources. **External** evidences for inspiration include such things as historical documentation of biblical people, places, and events, or archaeological artifacts that corroborate biblical statements or circumstances. **Internal** evidences are part of the warp and woof of the actual biblical fabric itself. These are self-authenticating phenomena from within the Sacred Volume that bear singular testimony to the fact that the very existence of the Holy Scriptures cannot be explained in any other way except to acknowledge that they are the result of an overriding, superintending, guiding Mind.

Critics, of course, have objected to the use of the Bible as a witness to its own inspiration. Dickson has pointed out correctly, however, that

> ...this contention is really unjust. One does not have a right to deny the authenticity of a document without considering the document itself. We would not deny Shakespeare's authorship of the Shakespearean plays without first considering their text. The Bible should at least be treated as just another book. Nevertheless, even this right is rejected by the prejudiced minds of some (1997, p. 328).

Clark H. Pinnock once observed:

> While insisting on their right to treat the Bible "like any other book" (vs. a book produced by man alone), some critics proceed to treat it like no other book, by bathing it in the acid solution of their skepticism and historical pessimism (1972, pp. 22-23, parenthetical item in orig.).

When the evidences for the Bible's inspiration are allowed to speak for themselves, however, the story they tell is totally in accord with the Bible's claims for its own inspiration. Consider, for example, the following.

The Unity of the Bible

The Bible exhibits a unity that–on purely human terms–is quite simply inexplicable. In order to appreciate that unity, one first must come to terms with how The Book was put together. The Bible was written by more than forty different men from practically every walk of life. Nehemiah was a royal cupbearer. Peter was a fisherman. Luke was a physician. Matthew was a tax collector. Solomon was a king. Moses was a shepherd. Paul was a tentmaker. Furthermore, these men wrote from almost every conceivable human condition. David wrote from heights of joy on the rolling, grassy hills of Judea. Paul wrote from pits of despair caused by Roman incarceration. They wrote in three languages (Hebrew, Aramaic, and Greek) from at least two continents (Europe and Asia) over a period of time that spanned approximately sixteen centuries (1500 B.C. to A.D. 100). And they covered topics as diverse as eschatology, soteriology, theology, psychology, geography, history, medicine, and many others.

All this being true, one might expect that so diverse a group of men, writing on so varied a group of subjects, over such a lengthy span of time, would have produced a book that would be a tangled mishmash of subjects more often than not marred by an incredible number of inconsistencies, errors, and incongruities. Yet this hardly is the case. In fact, quite the opposite is true. The Bible exhibits such astounding harmony, such consistent flow, and such unparalleled unity that it defies any purely naturalistic explanation. It is as if the Bible were a magnificent symphony orchestrated by a single Conductor. The "musicians" each may have played a different instrument, in a different place, at a different time. But when the talented Maestro combined the individual efforts, the end result was a striking masterpiece.

Consider this analogy. Suppose you assembled forty contemporary scholars with the highest academic training possible in a single field of study (e.g., forty academicians with terminal Ph.D. degrees in world history). Suppose, further, that you placed them in a room, and asked them to write a twenty-page paper on a single topic–the causes of World War II. What kind of consensus would be exhibited when all of their treatises were completed? Likely, the forty scholars would be unable to agree on all but a few points; their compositions would be recognized more for the **dis**agreements they contained than for the agreements. The Bible writers, by contrast, generally were not contemporaries. They worked independently, and the majority never even met another biblical writer. Most were not highly trained, and what training they did have certainly was not in the same field of study. Nor were they allowed to write on a single topic in which they already had an interest. Yet they produced a book that is unified from beginning to end. The books of 1 and 2 Chronicles and 1 and 2 Kings corroborate one another in numerous historical events. Joshua 1 verifies Deuteronomy 34. Judges 1:1 verifies Joshua 24:27-33. Ezra 1 verifies 2 Chronicles 36:22-23. Daniel refers to Jeremiah (Daniel 9:2). Ezekiel refers to Daniel (Ezekiel 28:3). And so on. This kind of unity, which is in evidence throughout the Sacred Volume, attests to the fact that there was a Superintending Intelligence behind it. So many writers, over so many years, covering so many themes, simply could not have been so harmonious by mere coincidence.

Each book of the Bible complements the others in a single unified **theme**. From Genesis to Revelation there is a marvelous unfolding of the general theme of man's fall from his holy estate, God's plan for his redemption (as carefully worked out across the centuries), the sinless life and atoning death of Jesus Christ, and the ultimate victory of the Christian system. In essence, the Bible is the story of one problem–sin–with one solution, Jesus Christ. In commenting on the Bible's remarkable unity of theme, Wayne Jackson has noted:

> The redemptive thread that runs through the Scriptures is wonderfully illustrated by a comparison between Genesis and Revelation, the first and last books of the holy canon. In Genesis the origin of the heavens and Earth is revealed (1:1), while in Revelation the consummation of earthly affairs is effected, and the old order is replaced by a "new heaven and earth" (i.e., heaven itself), spiritual in nature.... Man, who was originally perfect, but who fell into sin (Genesis 3:6), is, by virtue of his obedience, granted the opportunity to become perfect again (Revelation 7:14; 22:14). All of this is made possible, of course, by the seed of woman (Genesis 3:15), the offspring of David (Revelation 22:16), who, as a consequence of his sacrifice (Genesis 4:4), became an enthroned Lamb (Revelation 21:4). Thus, the sorrow of Eden (Genesis 3:16) will be transformed into the joy of heaven (Revelation 21:4), and that tree of life, from which our early parents were separated (Genesis 3:22-24), will be our glad possession once more (Revelation 22:14) [1991a, 11:1].

James Orr wrote:

> But the impartial mind cannot ignore the fact that in the writings which constitute our Bible there is a unity and progression, a guiding purpose, culminating in Jesus Christ and His redemption, a fullness and power of religious truth, which place them in a category, and compel the acknowlegement, of a unique origin answering to their unique character (1969, pp. 12- 13).

Each book of the Bible complements the others in a single, unified **plan**. In Genesis, there is the record of humanity's pristine origin and covenant relationship with God, followed by its tragic fall into a sinful state. But, a specific family line (the Hebrew nation) was selected to provide a remedy for this disaster (Genesis 12:1ff.; 22:18). Man needed to learn precisely what sin is, thus the books of Exodus through Deuteronomy document the giving of the law of God to Moses. Via a set of ordinances, sin would be defined and humanity would be illuminated regarding the price of rebellion against God (Romans 7:7,13; Galatians 3:19). The historical books of the Old Testament revealed mankind's inability to keep perfectly God's law system (Galatians 3:10), and therefore underscored the need for a Justifier–Someone to do for man what he could not do for himself. The prophets of the Old Testament heralded the arrival of that Savior (Luke 24:44); more than 300 prophecies focus on the promised Messiah.

After four silent centuries (the "inter-biblical era"), four Gospel writers described in great detail the arrival, and life's work, of the Justifier–Jesus of Nazareth. The books of Matthew, Mark, Luke, and John are carefully crafted accounts of the birth, life, death, and ultimate resurrection of the Son of God (John 20:30-31). Each emphasized different parts of Christ's ministry in order to relate the "good news" to Jews or Gentiles. Matthew directed his record primarily to the Jewish nation. Mark stressed the works of Jesus. Luke, being the only Gentile writer of a Bible book (except possibly the author of Job), wrote to Gentiles. John's primary purpose in writing was to produce faith.

The book of Acts was written to convey the means by which mankind was to appropriate God's saving grace. It is a historical record that instructs a person on how to become a Christian. It also teaches about how the church of Christ was established in Jerusalem, and how that same church flourished throughout the Roman Empire of the first century. The various epistles that follow the book of Acts in the English Bible were directions to individuals and churches on how to obtain, and maintain, spiritual maturity. Finally, the book of Revelation predicted (in symbolic fashion) the ultimate triumph of good over evil–acknowledging that Christians would win, and Satan would lose. To the careful reader, the unity of both theme and plan in the Bible are apparent.

The Factual Accuracy of the Bible

The Bible claims to be the inspired Word of God. Therefore, it should be accurate in whatever subject(s) it discusses, since God is not the Author of confusion and contradiction (1 Corinthians 14:33), but of truth (John 17:17). The factual accuracy of the Bible proves that it **is** accurate. Time and again the Bible's facts have withstood the test. Examples abound.

Numerous passages indicate that Moses wrote the Pentateuch (2 Chronicles 34:14; Ezra 6:18; Nehemiah 13:1; Exodus 17:14; John 5:46; Mark 12:26). Having been adopted by the royal family of Egypt, he would have had access to the finest schools, best tutors, and greatest libraries which that country had to offer, thus securing for himself an impressive education (see Acts 7:22). Yet Bible critics suggested that Moses could not have written the Pentateuch because the art of writing was not developed until well after his death (c. 1451 B.C.). This criticism, however, has been blunted by a veritable plethora of archaeological discoveries. In 1933, J.L. Starkey, who had studied under famed archaeologist W.M.F. Petrie, excavated the ancient city of Lachish, which had figured prominently in Joshua's conquest of Canaan (Joshua 10). Among other things, he unearthed a pottery water pitcher "inscribed with a dedication in eleven archaic letters, the earliest 'Hebrew' inscription known" (Wiseman, 1974, p. 705). Pfeiffer has noted: "The Old, or palaeo-Hebrew script is the form of writing which is similar to that used by the Phoenicians. A royal inscription of King Shaphatball of Gebal (Byblos) in this alphabet dates from about 1600 B.C." (1966, p. 33). In 1949, C.F.A. Schaeffer "found a tablet at Ras Shamra containing the thirty letters of the Ugaritic alphabet in their proper order. It was discovered that the sequence of the Ugaritic alphabet was the same as modern Hebrew, revealing that the Hebrew alphabet goes back at least 3,500 years" (Jackson, 1982, p. 32).

The Code of Hammurabi, (c. 2000-1700 B.C.) was discovered by a French archaeological expedition under the direction of Jacques de Morgan in 1901-1902 at the ancient site of Susa in what is now Iran. It was written on a piece of black diorite nearly eight feet high, and contained 282 sections. Free and Vos stated:

> The Code of Hammurabi was written several hundred years before the time of Moses (c. 1500-1400 B.C.).... This code, from the period 2000-1700 B.C., contains advanced laws similar to those in the Mosaic laws.... In view of this archaeological evidence, the destructive critic can no longer insist that the laws of Moses are too advanced for his time (1992, pp. 103,55).

The Code of Hammurabi established beyond doubt that writing was known hundreds of years before Moses. In fact, the renowned Jewish historian, Josephus, confirmed that Moses authored the Pentateuch (*Against Apion*, 1,8), and various non-Christian writers (Hecataeus, Manetha, Lysimachus, Eupolemus, Tacitus, Juvenal, and Longinus, to name only a few), credited Moses as having authored the first five books of the English Bible (see Rawlinson, 1877, pp. 254ff.).

In days of yore, detractors accused Isaiah of having made a historical mistake when he wrote of Sargon as king of Assyria (Isaiah 20:1). For years, this remained the sole historical reference–secular or biblical–to Sargon having been linked with the Assyrian nation. Thus, critics assumed Isaiah had erred. But in 1843, Paul Emile Botta, the French consular agent at Mosul, working with Austen Layard, unearthed historical evidence that established Sargon as having been exactly what Isaiah said he was–king of the Assyrians. At Khorsabad, Botta discovered Sargon's palace. Pictures of the find may be found in *Halley's Bible Handbook* (1962, p. 289). Apparently, from what scholars have been able to piece together from archaeological and historical records, Sargon made his capital successively at Ashur, Calah, Nineveh, and finally at Khorsabad, where his palace was constructed in the closing years of his reign (c. 706 B.C.). The walls of the palace were adorned quite intricately with ornate text that described the events of his reign. Today, an artifact from the palace—a forty-ton stone bull (slab)—is on display at the University of Chicago's Oriental Institute ("weighty" evidence indeed of Sargon's existence!). Isaiah had been correct all along. And the critics had been wrong—all along.

One of the most famous archaeologists of the last century was Sir William Ramsay, who disputed the accuracy of events recorded by Luke in the book of Acts. Ramsay believed those events to be little more than second-century, fictitious accounts. Yet after years of literally digging through the evidence in Asia Minor, Ramsay concluded that Luke was an exemplary historian. In the decades since Ramsay, other scholars have suggested that Luke's historical background of the New Testament is among the best ever produced. As Wayne Jackson noted:

> In Acts, Luke mentions thirty-two countries, fifty-four cities, and nine Mediterranean islands. He also mentions ninety-five persons, sixty-two of which are not named elsewhere in the New Testament. And his references, where checkable, are always correct. This is truly remarkable, in view of the fact that the political/territorial situation of his day was in a state of almost constant change. Only inspiration can account for Luke's precision (1991b, 27[1]:2).

Other Bible critics have suggested that Luke misspoke when he designated Sergius Paulus as proconsul of Cyprus (Acts 13:7). Their claim was that Cyprus was governed by a propraetor (also known as a consular legate), not a proconsul. Upon further examination, such a charge can be seen to be completely vacuous, as Thomas Eaves has documented.

> As we turn to the writers of history for that period, Dia Cassius (*Roman History*) and Strabo (*The Geography of Strabo*), we learn that there were two periods of Cyprus' history: first, it was an imperial province governed by a propraetor, and later in 22 B.C., it was made a senatorial province governed by a proconsul. Therefore, the historians support Luke in his statement that Cyprus was ruled by a proconsul, for it was between 40-50 A.D. when Paul made his first missionary journey. If we accept secular history as being true we must also accept Biblical history for they are in agreement (1980, p. 234).

The science of archaeology seems to have outdone itself in verifying the Scriptures. Famed archaeologist William F. Albright wrote: "There can be no doubt that archaeology has confirmed the substantial historicity of the Old Testament tradition" (1953, p. 176). Nelson Glueck, himself a pillar within the archaeological community, said: "It may be stated categorically that no archaeological discovery has ever controverted a Biblical reference. Scores of archaeological findings have been made which conform in clear outline or exact detail historical statements in the Bible" (1959, p. 31). Such statements, offered 30+ years ago, are as true today as the day they were made. Jerry Moffitt observed:

> Over thirty names (emperors, high priests, Roman governors, princes, etc.) are mentioned in the New Testament, and all but a handful have been verified. In every way the Bible accounts have been found accurate (though vigorously challenged). In no single case does the Bible let us down in geographical accuracy. Without one mistake, the Bible lists around forty-five countries. Each is accurately placed and named. About the same number of cities are named and no one mistake can be listed. Further, about thirty-six towns are mentioned, and most have been identified. Wherever accuracy can be checked, minute detail has been found correct–every time! (1993, p. 129).

The Hittites are mentioned over forty times in Scripture (Exodus 23:28; Joshua 1:4; et al.), and were so feared that on one occasion they caused the Syrians to flee from Israel (2 Kings 7:6). Yet critics suggested that Hittites were a figment of the Bible writers' imaginations, since no evidence of their existence had been located. But in the late 1800s, A.H. Sayce discovered inscriptions in Syria that he designated as Hittite. Then, in 1906, Hugh Winckler excavated Boghazkoy, Turkey and discovered that the Hittite capital had been located on that very site. His find was all the more powerful because of the more than 10,000 clay tablets that were found in the ancient city's library and that contained the society's law system –which eventually came to be known as the Hittite Code. Thus, Ira Price wrote of the Hittites:

> The lack of extra-biblical testimony to their existence led some scholars about a half-century ago to deny their historicity. They scoffed at the idea of Israel allying herself with such an unhistorical people as the Hittites, as narrated in 2 Kings vii.6. But those utterances have vanished into thin air (1907, pp. 75-76).

In his classic text, *Lands of the Bible*, J.W. McGarvey remarked:

> A fictitious narrative, located in a country with which the writer is not personally familiar, must either avoid local allusions or be found frequently in conflict with the peculiarities of place and of manners and customs. By this conflict the fictitious character of the narrative is exposed (1881, p. 375).

McGarvey then documented numerous instances in which the facts of the Bible can be checked, and in which it always passes the test. Are compass references accurate? Is Antioch of Syria actually "down" from Jerusalem, even though it lies to the north of the holy city (Acts 15:1)? Is the way from Jerusalem to Gaza "south" of Samaria (Acts 8:26)? Is Egypt "down" from Canaan (Genesis 12:10)? McGarvey went on to note that "in not a single instance of this kind has any of the Bible writers been found at fault" (p. 378). Further, as Jackson has commented:

> In 1790, William Paley, the celebrated Anglican scholar, authored his famous volume, *Horae Paulinae* (*Hours with Paul*). In this remarkable book, Paley demonstrated an amazing array of "undesigned coincidences" between the book of Acts and the epistles of Paul, which argue for the credibility of the Christian revelation. "These coincidences," said Paley, "which are often incorporated or intertwined in references and allusions, in which no art can be discovered, and no contrivance traced, furnish numerous proofs of the truth of both these works, and consequently that of Christianity" (1839 edition, p. xvi). In 1847, J.J. Blunt of Cambridge University released a companion volume titled, *Undesigned Coincidences in the Writings of Both the Old Testament and New Testament.* Professor Blunt argued that both Testaments contain numerous examples of "consistency without contrivance" which support the Scriptures' claim of a unified origin from a supernatural source, namely God (1884, p. vii) [1991a, pp. 2-3].

A sampling of the information within Paley's and Blunt's books provides startling evidence of the fact that the writers simply could not have "contrived" their stories. Often, the writers were separated from one another by centuries, yet their stories dovetail with astounding accuracy, and provide additional proof of the Bible's inspiration.

When Joseph was seventeen years old, he was sold into Egyptian slavery by his brothers. While serving in the house of an Egyptian named Potiphar, Joseph found himself the object of affection of Potiphar's wife, whose advances he rejected. Her anger aroused, she fabricated a story that resulted in Joseph's being thrown into prison where the king's captives were "bound" (Genesis 39:20). In the context of this passage, the word "bound" is of critical importance because hundreds of years after the fact the psalmist would state of Joseph: "His feet they hurt with fetters: He was laid in chains of iron" (Psalm 105:18). Contrivance–or consistency?

When Pharaoh stubbornly refused to release the Israelites from bondage, God rained down plagues on the Egyptian monarch and his people, including a plague of hail that destroyed the **flax** in the fields (Exodus 9:31). Eventually, the Israelites were released, traveled to the wilderness of Sinai, were found faithless in God's sight, and were forced to wander for four decades while everyone over the age of twenty perished (except for the houses of Joshua and Caleb–Numbers 14:29-30). Finally, however, the Hebrews were allowed to enter the promised land of Canaan. The arrival of the younger generation was exactly forty years after Moses had led them out of Egypt (Joshua 4:19), and thus shortly before the anniversary of that eighth plague which destroyed the flax. The book of Joshua mentions that their entrance into Canaan was near harvest time (3:15). Interestingly, when spies were sent to investigate the city of Jericho, the Bible notes that they were concealed by Rahab under drying stalks of **flax** upon the rooftop of her house (Joshua 2:6). Coincidence–or concordance?

In Exodus 1:11, the story is related of how the Israelites were forced to build the treasure cities of Pithom and Raamses for the Egyptian ruler. Exodus 5 records that, initially, the slaves made bricks containing straw, but later were forced to use stubble because Pharaoh ordered his taskmasters not to provide any more straw. Excavations at Pithom in 1883 by Naville, and in 1908 by Kyle, discovered that the lower layers of the structures were made of bricks filled with good, chopped straw. The middle layers had less straw with some stubble. The upper layers contained bricks that were made of pure clay, with no straw whatsoever (see Pfeiffer, 1966, p. 459). Contrivance–or correctness?

The Tell-el-Armarna Tablets (c. 1450 B.C.) record the custom of bowing down seven times when meeting a superior. Thus the statement in Genesis 33:3–"And he [Jacob] himself passed over before them, and bowed himself to the ground **seven times**, until he came near to his brother [Esau]"–is confirmed as an act of respect. Coincidence–or consistency?

In at least two places, the Old Testament speaks of the Horites (Genesis 14:6; 36:21). Until approximately 1925, no one ever had heard of the Horites. Once again, however, archaeology revealed the factual accuracy of the Bible. Around 1925, archaeological discoveries helped explain the existence of this formerly unknown nation. Free and Vos have commented that "Horite" derives from the Egyptian *Hurru*, which is "...a general term the Egyptians applied to southern Transjordan...," and that "...the Hebrews adopted it from the Egyptians" (1992, p. 66). Thus, both Egyptian and Hebrew cultures were intertwined with the Horites. Contrivance–or concordance?

On one occasion during His earthly ministry, Jesus miraculously provided a meal for more than 5,000 people. Mark records that the Lord seated the people upon the "green grass" (6:39). Such a statement agrees completely with John's reference to the fact that this event occurred near the time of the Passover (6:44), which occurs in the spring–exactly the time in Palestine when the grass should be green. Coincidence–or correctness?

In Acts 28:20, Luke described Paul's Roman imprisonment, and quoted the apostle as proclaiming: "...because of the hope of Israel I am bound with this chain." During this incarceration, Paul penned four important letters (Ephesians, Philippians, Colossians, and Philemon). In his epistle to the Ephesians, Paul alluded to his "chain" (6:20). In Philippians he referred to his "bonds" (1:7,13-14,17). Similarly, see the references to his "bonds" in Colossians 4:3 and Philemon 1:13. Coincidence–or consistency?

In his second letter to Timothy, Paul admonished the young man by stating that "...from a babe thou hast known the sacred writings which are able to make thee wise unto salvation through faith which is in Christ Jesus" (2 Timothy 3:15). The reference to the "sacred writings" is an allusion to the Old Testament. Since Timothy had known those writings from his earliest days, certainly it would be safe to suggest that his background was Jewish. As a matter of fact, the book of Acts states Timothy was "the son of a Jewess that believed, but his father was a Greek" (Acts 16:1). Of further interest is the fact that when Paul commended Timothy for his strong faith (2 Timothy 1:5), he alluded to the spirituality of both the young man's mother and grandmother, yet made no mention of Timothy's father. Coincidence–or concordance?

When Jesus died, His disciples desired to prepare His body for burial by embalming it. In his Gospel, John declared that the Jewish ruler, Nicodemus, brought a hundred pounds of spices (myrrh and aloes) for this purpose (19:39). It would be safe to conclude, therefore, that large quantities of these kinds of spices would be required for the embalming process. It is an undisputed fact of secular history that the Egyptians were experts in embalming. When Jacob died, the physicians of Egypt embalmed him (Genesis 50:2). Likewise, Joseph was embalmed upon his demise (50:26). The Egyptians required vast quantities of spices–like myrrh–for their embalming purposes. Not surprisingly, then, the Old Testament teaches that myrrh was imported by camel caravans into Egypt (Genesis 37:24). Contrivance–or inspiration?

In their book, *A General Introduction to the Bible*, Geisler and Nix wrote: "Confirmation of the Bible's accuracy in factual matters lends credibility to its claims when speaking on other subjects" (1986, p. 195). Indeed it does! After previewing many of the above facts, and others of a similar nature, Wayne Jackson concluded:

> The Bible critic is likely to trivialize these examples as they are isolated from one another. When, however, literally hundreds and hundreds of these incidental details are observed to perfectly mesh, one begins to suspect that what have been called "undesigned coincidences" (from the human vantage point) become very obvious cases of divinely designed harmony–tiny footprints that lead only to the conclusion that God was the guiding Force behind the composition of the Sacred Scriptures (1991a, 11:3).

The Prophecy of the Bible

One of the most impressive internal proofs of the Bible's inspiration is its prophetic utterances. Rex A. Turner Sr. suggested:

> Predictive prophecy is the highest evidence of divine revelation. The one thing that mortal man cannot do is to know and report future events in the absence of a train of circumstances that naturally suggest certain possibilities... (1989, p. 12).

If the Bible is inspired of God, then it should contain valid, predictive prophecy. In fact, the Bible's prophecy–completely foretold to the minutest detail, and painstakingly fulfilled with the greatest precision–has confounded its critics for generations. The Bible contains prophecies about individuals, lands, nations, and even the predicted Messiah.

Thomas H. Horne defined predictive prophecy as "a miracle of knowledge, a declaration or representation of something future, beyond the power of human sagacity to discern or to calculate" (1970, 1:272). The Bible confirms that definition:

> But the prophet, that shall speak a word presumptuously in my name, which I have not commanded him to speak, or that shall speak in the name of other gods, that same prophet shall die. And if thou say in thy heart, "How shall we know the word which Jeho-

> vah hath not spoken?," when a prophet speaketh in the name of Jehovah, if the thing follow not, nor come to pass, that is the thing which Jehovah hath not spoken: the prophet hath spoken it presumptuously, thou shalt not be afraid of him (Deuteronomy 18:20-22).

The prophet Isaiah based the credibility of his message on prophecy. To the promoters of idolatry in his day, he issued the following challenge: "Let them bring forth, and declare unto us what shall happen: declare ye the former things, what they are, that we may consider them, and know the latter end of them; or show us things to come" (Isaiah 41:22). His point was this: It is one thing to make the prediction; it is entirely another to see that prediction actually come true and be corroborated by subsequent history.

In order for a prophecy to be valid, it must meet certain criteria. First, it must be a specific, detailed declaration, as opposed to being nebulous, vague, or general in nature. Arthur Pierson wrote: "The particulars of the prophecy should be so many and minute that there shall be no possibility of accounting by shrewd guesswork for the accuracy of the fulfillment" (1913, pp. 75-76). Bernard Ramm has suggested: "The prophecy must be more than a good guess or a conjecture. It must possess sufficient precision as to be capable of verification by means of the fulfillment" (1971, p. 82).

Second, there must be a sufficient amount of time between the prophetic statement and its fulfillment. Suggestions about what "might" happen in the future do not qualify as prophetic pronouncements. Rather, the prophecy must precede the fulfillment in a significant fashion, and there must be no chance whatsoever of the prophet having the ability to influence the outcome.

Third, the prophecy must be stated in clear, understandable terms. Roger Dickson has noted: "Prophecies must be sufficiently clear in order for the observer to be able to link pronouncement with fulfillment. If a prophecy is not understandable enough so as to allow the observer to depict its fulfillment, then what good would the prophecy be?" (1997, p. 346).

Fourth, the prophecy must not have historical overtones. In other words, true prophecy should not be based on past (or current) societal or economic conditions. Pierson amplified this point by stating: "There should have been nothing in previous history which makes it possible to forecast a like event in the future" (1913, p. 75). Fifth, a clear, understandable, exact prophecy must have a clear, understandable, exact fulfillment. It is not enough to suggest that a certain event came true with a "high degree of probability." The fulfillment must be unmistakable, and must match the prophecy in every detail.

Two questions, then, are in order: (1) does the Bible employ predictive prophecy; and (2) if it does, can the predictive prophecy be proven true? The answer to both questions is a resounding, "Yes!" Further, the Bible's prophecy fits the above standards perfectly–each and every time. Consider just a few brief examples.

Within the Sacred Volume, numerous prophecies are presented regarding the rise, decline, and eventual fall of kings, cities, and even nations. (1) The Bible foretells the destruction of the city of Tyre with miraculous precision. Ezekiel predicted that Nebuchadnezzar, king of Babylon, would destroy the city (Ezekiel 26:7-8). Many nations were to come up against Tyre (26:3). The city would be leveled and scraped clean like a bare rock (26:4). The city's stones, timbers, and soil would be cast into the sea (26:12). The surrounding area would become a place for the spreading of fishermen's nets (26:5). And, finally, the city never would be rebuilt to its former glory (26:14).

History records that each of these predictions came true. Tyre, a coastal city from ancient times, had a somewhat unusual arrangement. In addition to the inland city, there was an island about three-fourth's of a mile offshore. Nebuchadnezzar besieged the mainland city in 586 B.C., but when he finally was able to inhabit the city in about 573 B.C., his victory was hollow. Unbeknownst to him, the inhabitants had vacated the city and moved to the island–a situation that remained virtually unchanged for the next 241 years. Then, in 332 B.C., Alexander the Great conquered the city–but not with ease. To get to the island, he literally had his army "scrape clean" the inland city of its debris, and he then used those materials (soil, stones, and timbers) to build a causeway to the island. While Alexander inflicted severe damage on the city, it still remained intact. In fact, it waxed and waned for the next 1,600 years until finally, in A.D. 1291, the Muslims thoroughly crushed Tyre.

The city never regained its once-famous position of wealth and power. The prophet Ezekiel looked 1,900 years into the future and predicted that Tyre would be a bald rock where fishermen gathered to open their nets. And that is exactly what history records as having happened (see Bromling, 1994, 14:96; Major, 1996, 16:93-95).

(2) During a time in the history of Israel in which God's people had delved deeply into idolatry, the prophet Isaiah foretold that God would raise up the Assyrians as His "rod of anger" in order to punish the disobedient Hebrews (Isaiah 10:5-6). But, Isaiah noted, after that had been accomplished, God would see to it that the Assyrians themselves were punished for their own wicked deeds (Isaiah 10:12,24-25).

Archaeology has revealed some impressive facts regarding this prophecy. Assyrian records, discovered in recent years, discuss the fact that in the reign of Hosea, king of Israel, Shalmanesar, ruler of Assyria, assaulted Samaria, the capital city of Israel. However, he died before completing the assault, which was taken up by his successor, Sargon, who captured the city (cf. 2 Kings 18:10). An Assyrian clay prism comments on the fact that 27,290 Israelite captives were taken in the conflict. Almost twenty-five years later, the Assyrian king Sennacherib once again invaded Palestine (2 Kings 18:13ff.). Archaeological records report that 46 Judean cities were seized and that 200,150 Israelites were captured. Jerusalem, however, was not conquered—a fact that is noteworthy since 2 Kings 19:32-34 predicted that Sennacherib would be unable to take the holy city.

The Taylor Cylinder, discovered at Nineveh in 1830, presents the history of the Assyrians' assault, and states that king Hezekiah of Judah was "shut up like a bird in a cage." But was Jerusalem itself spared? It was. And were the wicked Assyrians punished? They were. The account in 2 Kings 19:35 indicates that in one night God annihilated 185,000 Assyrian soldiers who had encircled Jerusalem. In addition, the prophecy stated that Sennacherib would return to his home and there fall by the sword (2 Kings 19:7). Some twenty years later, he was assassinated by his own sons, who smote him with the sword while he was worshiping pagan deities (Isaiah 37:37-38).

(3) King Josiah had his life's work foretold (his name even being provided within the prophetic utterance) **more than three hundred years before he was born** (1 Kings 13:2).

(4) But Josiah was not the only king who was called by name prior to birth. Cyrus, the man who would be the future king of Persia, likewise was called by name more than a century and a half prior to his birth (Isaiah 44:28; 45:1), and some of his activities as king were even foretold. As always, the prophecies of the biblical record came true in exacting detail.

(5) The Old Testament contains more than three hundred messianic prophecies. As Hugo McCord has said, "Testimony about Jesus was the chief purpose of prophecy. To him all the prophets gave witness (Acts 10:43)" (1979, p. 332). The

Prophesied One would be born of a woman (Genesis 3:15; Galatians 4:4), of the seed of Abraham (Genesis 22:18; Luke 3:34), of the tribe of Judah (Genesis 49:10; Hebrews 7:14), of the royal lineage of David (2 Samuel 7:12; Luke 1:32), in Bethlehem (Micah 5:2; Matthew 2:1), to the virgin Mary (Isaiah 7:14; Matthew 1:22), in order to bruise the head of Satan (Genesis 3:15; Galatians 4:4; Hebrews 2:12-14).

His Galilean ministry was foretold (Isaiah 9:1-2), and it was prophesied that a forerunner would announce His arrival (Isaiah 40:3; Matthew 3:1-3). He would appear during the days of the Roman reign (Daniel 2:44; Luke 2:1), while Judah still possessed her own king (Genesis 49:10; Matthew 2:22). He would be killed some 490 years after the command to restore Jerusalem at the end of the Babylonian captivity (457 B.C.), i.e., A.D. 30 (Daniel 9:24ff.). He was to be both human and divine; though born, He was eternal (Micah 5:2; John 1:1,14); though a man, He was Jehovah's "fellow" (Zechariah 13:7; John 10:30; Philippians 2:6). He was to be gentle and compassionate in His dealings with mankind (Isaiah 42:1-4; Matthew 12:15-21). He would submit perfectly to His heavenly Father (Psalm 40:8; Isaiah 53:11; John 8:29; 2 Corinthians 5:21; 1 Peter 2:22).

The prophecy was that He would be rejected and know grief (Isaiah 53:3), and be betrayed by a friend (Psalm 41:9) for thirty pieces of silver (Zechariah 11:12). He was (John 13:18; Matthew 26:15). He would be spit upon, and beaten (Isaiah 50:6; 53:5), and in death both His hands and His feet were to be pierced (Psalm 22:16). This is exactly what happened (Matthew 27:30; Luke 24:39). The Scriptures foretold that He would be numbered among criminals (Isaiah 53:12), which He was (Matthew 27:38). He would be mocked, not only with scornful words (Psalm 22:7-8), but with bitter wine (Psalm 22:18). And so He was (Matthew 27:39,48). Although He would die and be placed in a rich man's tomb (Isaiah 53:9; Matthew 27:57), His bones would not be broken (Psalm

34:20; John 19:33), and His flesh would not see corruption, because He would be raised from the dead (Psalm 16:10; Acts 2:22ff.), and eventually ascend into heaven (Psalm 110: 1-3; 45:6; Acts 1:9-10).

Time and again, biblical prophecies are presented and fulfilled with exacting detail. Jeremiah wrote: "When the word of the prophet shall come to pass, then shall the prophet be known, that Jehovah hath truly sent him" (28:9). Horne was absolutely correct when he wrote:

> The book which contains these predictions is stamped with the seal of heaven: a rich vein of evidence runs through the volume of the Old Testament; the Bible is true; infidelity is confounded forever; and we may address its patrons in the language of Saint Paul, "Behold, ye despisers, and wonder and perish!" (1970, 1:291).

The Scientific Foreknowledge of the Bible

Among the many intriguing proofs of the Bible's inspiration is its unique scientific foreknowledge. From anthropology to zoology, the Bible presents astonishingly accurate scientific information that the writers, on their own, simply could not have known. Henry Morris has suggested: "One of the most arresting evidences of the inspiration of the Bible is the great number of scientific truths that have lain hidden within its pages for thirty centuries or more, only to be discovered by man's enterprise within the last few centuries or even years" (1969, p. 5). In her book, *Science in the Bible*, Jean S. Morton commented:

> Many scientific facts, which prove the infallibility of Scripture, are tucked away in its pages. These proofs are given in nonscientific language; nevertheless, they substantiate the claims of authenticity of the Holy Scriptures.... In some cases, scientific concepts have been known through the ages, but these concepts are mentioned in a unique manner in Scripture. In other

> cases, scientific topics have been mentioned hundreds or even thousands of years before man discovered them (1978, p. 10).

Space limitations prohibit an in-depth examination of the Bible's scientific foreknowledge, but I would like to mention a few of the more prominent examples.

From the Field of Astronomy

1. Isaiah, in speaking of God, stated (40:22): "It is he who sitteth upon the circle of the earth." The Hebrew word Isaiah used for "circle" is the word *khug*, which means literally something with "roundness," a "sphere." But, of course, the people of Isaiah's day thought the Earth was flat. And that was the concept of the many generations of people who followed Isaiah. Later, it was discovered that the Earth was not flat; rather it was a *khug* (circle). Isaiah had been correct all along, even when the people of his day emphatically stated the opposite. How did Isaiah know the Earth to be a sphere? A lucky guess?

[NOTE: In recent years, some have suggested that Isaiah's statement contains no foreknowledge, since in chapter 40 he was dealing solely with the subject of God's sovereignty, and therefore it was not his intent to teach "scientific truths" (cf. England, 1983, pp. 135ff.). I repudiate such a claim. There is no doubt that Isaiah's treatise is dealing with the sovereign nature of the Israelite God. Chapter 40 is, in fact, one of the most beautiful and stirring passages in the Bible dealing with that very subject. At the same time, however, Isaiah did set forth a "scientific truth" while acknowledging an important "spiritual truth." One does not preclude the other. Isaiah made two points: (1) God **is** sovereign; and (2) the Earth **is** a sphere (*khug*). How could Isaiah have known either, unless God had revealed them both?]

2. Psalm 19:5-6 contains several interesting scientific facts. In speaking of the Sun, the psalmist suggested that "his going forth is from the end of the heaven, and his circuit unto the

ends of it; and there is nothing hid from the heat thereof." For years, Bible critics scoffed at Bible believers, stating that this verse taught the false concept of geocentricity (i.e., the Sun revolves around the Earth). Then it was discovered that the Sun, not the Earth, was the center of our solar system. People subsequently felt that the Sun was stationary, with the Earth revolving around it.

Only fairly recently has it been discovered that rather than being fixed in space, the Sun actually is in an orbit of its own. In fact, it is estimated to be moving through space at the rate of 600,000 miles per hour, in an orbit so large it would take approximately 220,000,000 years to complete just one orbit. How did the psalmist portray such accurate statements–when people of this day, and for years afterward, taught that just the opposite was true? And, by the way, there is another gem packed away in these two verses. The psalmist hinted at the fact that the Sun is the source of energy for the Earth ("and there is nothing hid from the heat thereof"). An amazing statement, is it not, considering when it was written, and by whom?

3. Concerning light and darkness, the Lord asked Job: "Where is the way to the dwelling of the light? And as for darkness, where is the place thereof?" (38:19). Light is said to travel in a "way" (Hebrew, *derek*), which is literally a traveled path or road (cf. Genesis 16:7), whereas darkness is said to be a "place" (Hebrew, *maxim*) which means a place, a spot, as standing (cf. Genesis 1:9; 28:11). Until the seventeenth century, it was believed that light was transmitted instantaneously. Then Sir Isaac Newton suggested that light is composed of small particles that travel in a straight line. Christian Huygens proposed the wave theory of light, and Olaus Roemer measured the velocity of light as evinced by its delay while traveling through space. Scientists now know that light is a form of energy called radiant energy, and that it travels in electromagnetic waves in a straight line at the speed of over 186,000

miles per second (660 million miles per hour). For example, it takes about eight minutes for light to travel its "path" from the Sun to the Earth.

Scientists use the speed of light to measure distances in our vast Universe. Our solar system is said to be about 26,000 light-years from the edge of the Milky Way Galaxy. [A light year is the distance that light travels in a vacuum in one year (approximately 5.88 trillion miles). Distances expressed in light-years represent the time that light would take to cross that distance. For example, it would take 26,000 years, traveling at the speed of light, to go from the edge of the Milky Way Galaxy to our solar system.] Some evolutionists, who deny the chronological data found in the Bible, have suggested that light, which spans the distances from stars to us, proves the Universe is billions of years old. But in so doing, they have overlooked the fact that God created the heavenly lights already in place (Genesis 1:14-16) to serve as a "witness" of His infinite power and for man's benefit (Psalm 19:1). God, in making His perfect, mature Universe, formed the stars so that their light could be seen on Earth.

Jehovah also inquired of Job? "By what way is light parted?" (38:24). The word "parted" is from the Hebrew *halaq*, meaning to divide, allot, apportion (cf. Numbers 26:53). Though the Lord simply may have been asking the patriarch if he knew how light is distributed on Earth, nonetheless it is an amazing scientific fact that light literally can be parted. When a narrow beam of sunlight passes at a slant into a triangular, transparent prism, the sunlight is broken into a band of seven colored lights called a spectrum. Sir Isaac Newton eventually discovered this, yet the writer of the book of Job knew it first.

From the Field of Oceanography

1. Long ago, Solomon wrote, "All the rivers run into the sea, yet the sea is not full; unto the place whither the rivers go, thither they go again" (Ecclesiastes 1:7). This statement, con-

sidered by itself, may not seem profound at first glance. But when considered with additional evidence and other biblical passages, it becomes all the more remarkable. For example, the Mississippi River, when moving at normal speed, dumps approximately **6,052,500 gallons** of water **per second** into the Gulf of Mexico. And that is just one river! Where, pray tell, does all that water go? The answer, of course, lies in the hydrologic cycle so well illustrated in the Bible. Ecclesiastes 11:3a states that "if the clouds be full of rain, they empty themselves upon the earth." Amos 9:6b tells us that "He... calleth for the waters of the sea, and poureth them out upon the face of the earth; the Lord is His name." The idea of a complete water cycle was not fully understood or accepted until the sixteenth and seventeenth centuries. The first substantial evidence came from the experiments of Pierre Perrault and Edme Mariotte. These scientists demonstrated that the flow of the Seine River could be accounted for by precipitation. Astronomer Edmund Halley also contributed valuable data to the concept of a complete water cycle. More than 2,000 years prior to their work, however, the Scriptures had indicated a water cycle. How?

2. Job was asked by God (38:16), "Hast thou entered into the springs of the sea? Or hast thou walked in the recesses of the deep?" The Hebrew word for "recesses" (or "trenches") refers to that which is "hidden, and known only by investigation." What were these "recesses of the deep" (the Hebrew word for "deep" is the word for seas or oceans)? Man, in previous centuries, considered the seashore as nothing but a shallow, sandy extension that moved gently from one continent to another. Then, in 1873 a team of British scientists working in the Pacific Ocean found a "recess" 5½ miles deep. Later, another team of researchers discovered another trench 35,800 feet deep (over 6 miles down). Trenches now are known to exist in all three major oceans, but the Pacific Ocean is unique in that it has a semi-continuous peripheral belt of

trenches and deep-sea troughs. Extensive scientific studies have been conducted on the Marianas Trench off the coast of Guam. One bathyscaph, the *Trieste*, has traveled down almost seven miles into that trench. The best-known trench is likely the one off the coast of Puerto Rico, with its deepest point known as the Milwaukee Depth. How did Job know about these "recesses in the deep," when we did not discover them for millennia? A lucky guess?

3. God told Noah (Genesis 6:15) to build an ark that measured 300 cubits in length, 50 cubits in width, and 30 cubits in height–which is a ratio of 30 to 5 to 3, length to breadth to height. Until around 1858, the ark was the largest seagoing vessel of which we have any written record. Using the most conservative estimate available for a cubit (approximately 17½ to 18 inches), the ark would have been roughly 450 feet long (one-and-a-half football fields) and would have contained approximately 1.5 million cubic feet of space. In 1844, when Isambard K. Brunnel built his giant ship the *Great Britain*, he constructed it to almost the exact dimensions of the ark –30:5:3. As it turns out, these dimensions are the perfect ratio for a huge boat built for seaworthiness and not for speed. Obviously the ark was not built for speed; it had nowhere to go! In fact, shipbuilders during World War II used that 30:5:3 ratio to build the boat (the *S.S. Jeremiah O'Brien*) that eventually was nicknamed "the ugly duckling"–a huge, barge-like boat (with the same ratio as the ark) built to carry tremendous amounts of cargo. How did Noah know the perfect seagoing ratio to use in building the ark? Upon whose knowledge did he draw? Brunnel and others like him had many generations of shipbuilding knowledge upon which to draw, but Noah's craft literally was the first of its kind.

From the Field of Physics

1. Moses (Genesis 2:1) stated: "And the heavens and the earth were finished, and all the host of them." This is an ex-

tremely interesting assessment of the situation, because Moses chose the Hebrew past definite tense for the verb "finished," indicating an action completed in the past, not re-occurring in the future. Moses stated that the creation was "finished"–once and for all. That is exactly what the First Law of Thermodynamics states. This law (often referred to as the Law of Conservation of Energy/Matter) states that neither matter nor energy can be created or destroyed. It was because of this law that Fred Hoyle's "Steady State" (or "Continuous Creation") Theory was discarded several years ago. Hoyle stated that at points in the Universe called "irtrons," matter was being created constantly. But the First Law states just the opposite. The Bible says that God "ended His work which He had made" (Genesis 2:2). As Henry Morris has suggested: "This is the most universal and certain of all scientific principles, and it states conclusively that, so far as empirical observation has shown, there is **nothing** now being created anywhere in the known universe" (1974, p. 235, emp. in orig.).

It is because God has finished His creation that nothing now is being created. But, as a corollary to that, why is it that nothing is being destroyed? This is the second half of the statement of the law. Matter and/or energy may change form, but in the end the total amount of energy in the Universe remains the same. Nothing is being destroyed, even though its form may change. Once again, the answer can be found in the science of the Bible. Nehemiah provided a portion of the answer when he stated: "Thou hast made heaven, the heaven of heavens, with all their host, the earth, and all things that are therein, the seas, and all that is therein, and thou preservest them all" (9:6). Hebrews 1:3 points out that God "upholds all things by the word of His power." If God is upholding it, then man will not destroy it. Other verses make that clear in this regard (cf. Isaiah 40:26, Ecclesiastes 3:14, and 2 Peter 3:7). Thus, we see that the biblical writers penned accurate scientific statements long before such statements were even known to be scientific. How? Just a lucky guess?

2. In three different places in the Bible (Hebrews 1:11; Isaiah 51:6; Psalm 102:26) the indication is given that the Earth, like a garment, is wearing out. This, of course, is exactly what the Second Law of Thermodynamics states. This law, also known as the Law of Increasing Entropy, governs all processes; there is not a single known exception. The law states that as time progresses, entropy increases. Entropy is the scientific word which simply means that things become more disorderly, more random, more unstructured. In other words, a flower blooms, fades, and dies. A child grows into adolescence, adulthood, senility, and dies. The house we build today, in 250 years will be a heap of junk. The car we buy today, given 30 or 40 years, will rust and fall apart. Everything is running down. Everything is wearing out. Energy is becoming less available for work. Eventually then (theoretically speaking) the Universe, left to itself, will experience a "heat death"–i.e., a time when no more energy is available for use. We did not discover these things until fairly recently, yet the Bible writers portrayed them accurately thousands of years ago. What was the source of their knowledge?

From the Field of Medicine

1. Moses told the Israelites (Leviticus 17:11-14) that "the life of the flesh is in the blood." He was correct. Because the red blood cells can carry oxygen (due to hemoglobin in the cells), life is made possible. In fact, the human red blood cells carry approximately 270,000,000 molecules of hemoglobin per cell (see Perutz, 1964, pp. 64-65). If there were any less, there would not be enough residual oxygen to sustain life after, say, a hard sneeze or a hefty pat on the back.

We know today that the "life of the flesh is in the blood." Unfortunately, we did not know that in George Washington's day. How did the "father of our country" die? We bled him to death (see Havron, 1981, p. 62). People believed that the blood was where evil "vapors" were found, and that getting rid of the blood would make a person well again. Today, of course, we know that is not true. Think of how often blood transfusions have made life possible for those who otherwise would have died. Today we know the truth of the matter. But how did the biblical writer know it?

2. Genesis 3:15 teaches plainly that both the male and the female possess the "seed of life." This was not the commonly held position in Moses' day, however. Nor was it the commonly held position just a few centuries ago. Several writers of days gone by, including some of Moses' day, felt that only the male possessed the seed of life, and that a woman actually was little more than a "glorified incubator." One writer even went so far as to suggest that the male seed could be deposited in warm mud, and the end result would be the same as placing it in a woman's womb. But Moses spewed forth no such nonsense. Rather, he stated the truth of the matter. But how did he know? Upon whose knowledge of such facts did he draw?

3. Leviticus 17:15 teaches that an animal that has died **naturally** is not to be eaten. Moses obviously was highly trained in public health procedures, for he certainly knew that of which he spoke. Today, it is against local, state, and federal public health laws to take an animal that has died naturally to a slaughterhouse in order to be prepared for human consumption. What if the animal had died of rabies, anthrax, brucellosis, or a similar disease? Obviously, it would not be suitable for human consumption because if the animal died, **something** was wrong. Even today this practice is one of our most basic public health standards. But how did Moses possess such knowledge?

4. While the Old Testament placed no restrictions on the eating of fruits and vegetables, it did set strict limitations on the eating of certain meats. Among land animals, only those that had a split hoof and chewed the cud were approved as edible (Leviticus 11:3). Of the water-living animals, only

those with fins and scales were acceptable (Leviticus 11:9; of interest is the fact that poisonous fish have no scales). Birds of prey were prohibited, as were almost all insects. But perhaps the best known among these biblical injunctions was eating the meat of a pig. To the Jew, pork was considered unclean, and thus was inedible.

Today, we know there is good scientific reasoning behind such a prohibition. The pig is a scavenger, and will eat almost anything. In so doing, on occasion it ingests a parasite, *Trichinella spiralis*, which is the cause of trichinosis in humans. Left untreated, this disease can be debilitating and even deadly. Pigs also are known carriers (as intermediate hosts) of the tapeworm *Taenia solium*, and of the parasite *Echinococcus granulosis*, which causes tumors in the liver, lungs, and other parts of the body. Raw or undercooked pork can be quite dangerous when consumed by humans. Pigs can provide safe meat if they are fed properly and if the muscle tissue is cooked correctly. But such conditions often did not prevail in ancient times.

Were the Israelites "ahead of their times" in regard to their extensive public health and personal hygiene laws? Archaeologists admit that they have yet to find civilizations as ancient as the Israelites with rules and regulations that could rival those of the Jewish people in regard to complexity and scientific accuracy. The Egyptians, for example, were brilliant in many respects when it came to their medical technology. Yet the Jews had access to this kind of information (and much more) that not even the Egyptians possessed. Interestingly, even today in some countries (like Germany) raw pork is considered a delicacy–in spite of the knowledge we possess about the potential dangers of eating it.

5. In Deuteronomy 23:12-14, Moses instructed the Israelites always to bury human waste products. Today, of course, with centuries of experience behind us, we know that this is an excellent hygienic practice. But the common course of ac-

tion in Moses' day, and for centuries to follow, was to dump waste products in any convenient place. History has recorded the folly of this kind of action.

In Europe during the Middle Ages, "black plague" swept over the continent on two different occasions, slaughtering more than 13 million people in the process. [Philip Ziegler's fascinating book, *The Black Death* (1997), recounts in excruciating detail the horror of the two epidemics.] Europeans routinely dumped waste of all kinds out their windows and into the public streets where decomposition took place and microorganisms flourished.

One of those microorganisms–the one we know today as *Yersinia pestis*–grew in the waste products and contaminated the fleas associated with those waste products. The fleas, using rats as their hosts, subsequently traveled into the people's houses. Once inside a dwelling, the fleas then jumped from the rats onto the humans, biting them and infecting them with the plague organism. As this cycle was repeated over and over, millions perished. Yet if the people simply had obeyed God's injunction, as given by Moses to the Israelites, all of the death and horror of not one, but two separate epidemics could have been avoided. How did Moses know to instruct the Israelites regarding such public health hygiene laws, when none of the nations surrounding God's people enlisted such practices–and would not for centuries?

6. In Genesis 17:12, God commanded Abraham to circumcise newborn males on the **eighth** day. But why day eight? In humans, blood clotting is dependent upon three factors: (a) platelets; (b) vitamin K; and (c) prothrombin. In 1935, professor H. Dam proposed the name "vitamin K" for the factor that helped prevent hemorrhaging in chicks. We now realize that vitamin K is responsible for the production (by the liver) of prothrombin. If the quantity of vitamin K is deficient, there will be a prothrombin deficiency and hemorrhaging may occur.

Interestingly, it is only on the fifth to seventh days of a newborn's life that vitamin K (produced by the action of bacteria in the intestinal tract) is present in adequate quantities. Vitamin K–coupled with prothrombin–causes blood coagulation, which is important in any surgical procedure. One classic medical text, *Holt Pediatrics*, corroborates the fact that a newborn infant has

> ...peculiar susceptibility to bleeding between the second and fifth days of life.... Hemorrhages at this time, though often inconsequential, are sometimes extensive; they may produce serious damage to internal organs, especially to the brain, and cause death from shock and exsanguination (1953, pp. 125-126).

Obviously, then, if vitamin K is not produced in sufficient quantities until days five through seven, it would be wise to postpone any surgery until sometime after that. But why did God specify day **eight**?

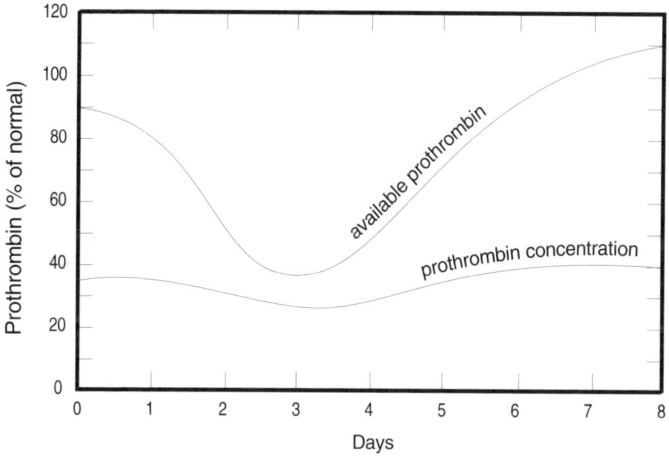

On the eighth day, the amount of prothrombin present actually is **elevated above 100 percent of normal**. In fact, day eight is the only day in the male's life in which this will be the case under normal conditions. If surgery is to be performed, day eight is the perfect day to do it.

S.I. McMillen, the renowned medical doctor who wrote *None of These Diseases*, stated concerning this information:

> ...as we congratulate medical science for this recent finding, we can almost hear the leaves of the Bible rustling. They would like to remind us that four thousand years ago, when God **initiated** circumcision with Abraham, He said "And he that is eight days old shall be circumcised...." Abraham did not pick the eighth day after many centuries of trial-and-error experiments. Neither he nor any of his company from the ancient city of Ur in the Chaldees had ever been circumcised. It was a day picked by the Creator of vitamin K (1963, p. 21, emp. in orig.).

The medical information employed by Abraham, and confirmed by Moses, was accurate scientifically then, and remains so to this very day. No culture around the Israelites possessed such scientific acumen, which, by the way, was years ahead of its time. How, then, did Abraham and Moses come to know the best time for circumcision, unless, of course, this particular fact was revealed to them by God, and recorded in His Word through inspiration?

From the Field of Biology

1. Moses stated (Genesis 1:11,12,21,24) that things reproduce "after their kind." This, of course, is no surprise to us today because we understand genetics and the laws of heredity which ensure that things do indeed reproduce "after their kind." If a farmer plants corn seed, he knows full well that he will not be harvesting wheat. If he breeds a bull to a heifer, he knows that the end result will not be a baby colt. Corn produces corn; cows produce cows. Why is this the case? It is because all living things reproduce "after their kind." Even today, in nature these things hold true. But how did Moses know that–long years before the science of genetics (which came into existence only around 1900) was discovered?

2. Paul stated that it is God who giveth all life (Acts 17:25). For centuries, men have been trying to "create life" through processes of spontaneous generation. Even though scientists such as Spallanzani, Redi, Pasteur, and hundreds of others have proven time and again that spontaneous generation is impossible, evolutionists still keep on trying. To date, however, no one has "created" life. They do well, in fact, even to get one of the elementary "building blocks"–amino acids. Yet Paul knew long ago that it was God who gives life. Just a lucky guess?

3. Paul also stated that there are **four** fleshes–those of men, beasts, birds and fishes (1 Corinthians 15:39). Today even evolutionists accept this fact of science. These fleshes are indeed different in their biochemical make-up. But how did Paul, an itinerant preacher of the first century A.D., know this?

From the Field of Archaeology

1. The Moabite Stone, discovered in 1868 by a German missionary, was cut in 850 B.C., in the reign of Mosha, king of Moab. It tells of his being subjected to the Israelites. It also mentions that Omri, the captain of the Israelite host, was made king in that day. The Scriptures speak of that very event in 1 Kings 16:16. With every scoop of dirt that the spade overturns, archaeology proves biblical statements to be factual.

2. The Bible plainly speaks of a king by the name of Belshazzar (Daniel 5:22; 7:1; 8:1). It was common practice for Bible critics to ridicule the Bible regarding its references concerning Belshazzar, because secular records never had been found that substantiated what the Bible said. Then, in 1876, Sir Henry Rawlinson discovered more than 2,000 tablets concerning Babylon. They disclosed records of a man named Belshazzar who, in the absence of his father Nabonidus, became king. The Bible had been right all along.

The incredible accuracy of the Bible's science is yet another example of God's superintending guidance, and one that provides an impressive proof of its inspiration.

CONCLUSION

Those who have set their face against God have railed against the Bible for generations. King Jehoiakim took a penknife, slashed the Old Testament Scriptures to pieces, and then tossed them into an open fire (Jeremiah 36:22-23). During the Middle Ages, attempts were made to keep the Bible from the common man. In fact, those caught translating or distributing the Scriptures frequently were subjected to imprisonment, torture, and even death. Centuries later, the French skeptic Voltaire boasted that "within fifty years, the Bible no longer will be discussed among educated people." His braggadocio notwithstanding, the Bible still is being discussed among educated people, while the name of Voltaire languishes in relative obscurity.

Like the blacksmith's anvil–which wears out many hammers but itself remains unaffected–the Bible wears out the skeptics' innocuous charges, all the while remaining unscathed. John Clifford (1836-1923), a Baptist minister and social reformer, wrote:

> Last eve I passed beside a blacksmith's door,
> And heard the anvil ring the vesper chime;
> Then looking, I saw upon the floor,
> Old hammers, worn with beating years of time.
> "How many anvils have you had," said I,
> "To wear and batter all these hammers so?"
> "Just one," said he, and then with twinkling eye;
> "The anvil wears the hammers out, ye know."
> And so, thought I, the anvil of God's Word,
> For ages skeptic blows have beat upon;
> Yet though the noise of falling blows was heard
> The anvil is unharmed...the hammers gone.

Governments come and go. Nations rise and fall. People live and die. Jesus warned that "heaven and earth shall pass away" (Matthew 24:35), but went on to note that "my words shall not pass away." Isaiah wrote: "The grass withereth, the flower fadeth; but the word of our God shall stand forever" (40:8). I believe it is fitting that we close this study with these words from Kenny Barfield's book, *Why the Bible is Number 1*:

> We have seen how the biblical materials are unique. They are no run-of-the-mill religious writings, but–quite the contrary–reveal a remarkable understanding of the universe.... How did the biblical writers manage to avoid the erroneous world views of their contemporaries? What made these men capable of producing painstakingly accurate scientific statements far in advance of their actual discovery? We want answers to those important questions....
>
> One answer has been suggested by the biblical writers themselves. If their materials are so radically different from other sources, surely we must listen to their explanation. Rather than finding confusion or uncertainty in their ranks, we find calm unanimity.
>
> They refused to be called geniuses and scorned personal glory. Even more significant, they denied having figured it out for themselves. In fact, there is reason to believe that they never really understood the far-reaching implications of the words they wrote.
>
> Humbly, without a dissenting voice, these writers gave credit to a superior being. One of their favorite phrases was: "This is the Word of God." They sensed a far-greater intelligence behind this universe than that of any mortal. They stood in awe before that wisdom and power. They even wrote words on their papyri and scrolls that made little earthly sense. "All Scripture is given by inspiration of God." It was the only answer they ever gave.

It is the thesis of this study that one must simply look at the trademark, the signature of authorship.... Unless we can devise a more suitable explanation, it seems reasonable to believe that the seemingly incongruous wisdom was placed in the Bible by an intelligence far greater than that of man. That intelligence is God's alone (1988, pp. 182,184-185).

REFERENCES

Albright, William F. (1953), *Archaeology and the Religion of Israel* (Baltimore, MD: Johns Hopkins University Press).

Barfield, Kenny (1988), *Why the Bible is Number 1* (Grand Rapids, MI: Baker).

Baxter, Batsell Barrett (1971), *I Believe Because* (Grand Rapids, MI: Baker).

Blunt, J.J. (1884), *Undesigned Coincidences in the Writings of the Old and New Testaments* (London: John Murray).

Bromling, Brad T. (1994), "Prophetic Precision," *Reason & Revelation*, 14:96, December.

Chafer, L.S. (1926), *Major Bible Themes* (Grand Rapids, MI: Zondervan).

Cheyne, T.K., ed. (1899), *Encyclopedia Biblica* (London: A&C Black).

Dickson, Roger E. (1997), *The Dawn of Belief* (Winona, MS: Choate).

Eaves, Thomas F. (1980), "The Inspired Word," *Great Doctrines of the Bible*, ed. M.H. Tucker (Knoxville, TN: East Tennessee School of Preaching).

England, Donald (1983), *A Scientist Examines Faith and Evidence*, (Delight, AR: Gospel Light).

Free, Joseph P. and Howard F. Vos (1992), *Archaeology and Bible History* (Grand Rapids, MI: Zondervan).

Geisler, Norman and William E. Nix (1986), *A General Introduction to the Bible* (Chicago, IL: Moody).

Glueck, Nelson (1959), *Rivers in the Desert: A History of the Negev* (New York: Farrar, Strauss, and Cudahy).

Goodpasture, B.C. (1970), "Inspiration of the Bible," *The Church Faces Liberalism*, ed. T.B. Warren (Henderson, TN: Freed-Hardeman College).

Halley, H.H. *Halley's Bible Handbook* (Grand Rapids, MI: Zondervan).

Havron, Dean (1981), "Curious Cure-Alls" *Science Digest*, 89[8]:62, September.

Holt, L.E. and R. McIntosh (1953), *Holt Pediatrics* (New York: Appleton-Century-Crofts), twelfth edition.

Horne, Thomas H. (1970 edition), *An Introduction to the Critical Study and Knowledge of the Holy Scriptures* (Grand Rapids, MI: Baker).

Jackson, Wayne (1974), *Fortify Your Faith* (Stockton, CA: Courier Publications).

Jackson, Wayne (1982), *Biblical Studies in the Light of Archaeology* (Montgomery, AL: Apologetics Press).

Jackson, Wayne (1991a), "Bible Unity–An Argument for Inspiration," *Reason & Revelation*, 11:1-3, January.

Jackson, Wayne (1991b), "The Holy Bible–Inspired of God," *Christian Courier*, 27[1]:1-3, May.

Jackson, Wayne (1995), "The Case for the Existence of God–Part III," *Reason & Revelation*, 15:49-55, July.

Lindsell, Harold (1976), *The Battle for the Bible* (Grand Rapids, MI: Zondervan).

Major, Trevor (1996), "The Fall of Tyre," *Reason & Revelation*, 16:93-95, December.

McCord, Hugo (1979), "Internal Evidences of the Bible's Inspiration," *The Holy Scriptures*, ed. Wendell Winkler (Fort Worth, TX: Winkler Publications).

McGarvey, J.W. (1881), *Lands of the Bible* (Philadelphia, PA: Lippincott).

McMillen, S.I. (1963), *None of These Diseases* (Old Tappan, NJ: Revell).

Merideth, Noel (1972), "The Bible and Theories of Inspiration," *The Bible Versus Liberalism*, ed. W.A. Bradfield (Henderson, TN: Freed- Hardeman College).

Moffitt, Jerry (1993), "Arguments Used to Establish an Inerrant, Infallible Bible," *Biblical Inerrancy*, ed. Jerry Moffitt (Portland, TX: Portland Church of Christ).

Morris, Henry M. (1969), *The Bible and Modern Science* (Chicago, IL: Moody).

Morris, Henry M. (1974), *Many Infallible Proofs* (San Diego, CA: Creation-Life Publishers).

Morton, Jean S. (1978), *Science in the Bible* (Chicago, IL: Moody).

Orr, James (1969), *Revelation and Inspiration* (Chicago, IL: Moody).

Paley, William (1839), *The Works of William Paley* (Edinburgh: Thomas Nelson).

Perutz, H.F. (1964), *Scientific American*, pp. 64-65, November.

Pfeiffer, Charles F. (1966), *The Biblical World* (Grand Rapids, MI: Baker).

Pierson, Arthur T. (1913), *The Scriptures: God's Living Oracles* (London: Revell).

Pink, Arthur (1976 reprint), *The Divine Inspiration of the Bible* (Grand Rapids, MI: Baker).

Pinnock, Clark (1972), *A Defense of Biblical Infallibility* (Grand Rapids, MI: Baker).

Price, Ira (1907), *The Monuments and the Old Testament* (Philadelphia, PA: American Baptist Publication Society).

Ramm, Bernard H. (1971), *Protestant Christian Evidences* (Chicago, IL: Moody).

Rawlinson, George (1877), *Historical Evidences of the Truth of the Scripture Records* (New York: Sheldon & Company).

Ridenour, Fritz (1967), *Who Says God Created?* (Glendale, CA: Gospel Light).

Thompson, Bert (1981), "Science in the Bible," *Reason & Revelation*, 1:33-36, September.

Thompson, Bert (1995a), "The Case for the Existence of God –Part I," *Reason & Revelation*, 15:33-38, May.

Thompson, Bert (1995b), "The Case for the Existence of God –Part II," *Reason & Revelation*, 15:41-47, June. [See Jackson, 1995, for Part III.]

Thompson, Bert (1997), "In Defense Of...Christ's Deity," *Reason & Revelation*, 17:89-94, December.

Thompson, Bert (1998a), "In Defense Of...Christ's Church," *Reason & Rev*elation, 18:1-5, January.

Thompson, Bert (1998b), "In Defense Of...God's Plan of Salvation," *Reason & Revelation*, 18:17-22, March.

Thompson, Bert (1999), *My Sin, My Sovereign, My Salvation* (Montgomery, AL: Apologetics Press).

Thompson, Bert (2000), *Rock Solid Faith: How to Build It* (Montgmery, AL: Apologetics Press).

Thompson, Bert and Wayne Jackson (1992), *A Study Course in Christian Evidences* (Montgomery, AL: Apologetics Press).

Turner, Rex A. Sr. (1989), *Systematic Theology* (Montgomery, AL: Alabama Christian School of Religion).

Wiseman, D.J. (1974), *The New Bible Dictionary*, ed. J.D. Douglas (Grand Rapids, MI: Eerdmans).

Woods, Guy N. (no date), *The Case for Verbal Inspiration* [a tract], (Shreveport, LA: Lambert).

Ziegler, Philip (1997), *The Black Death* (London: Folio Society).

[AUTHOR'S NOTE: I would like to thank my friend and colleague, Wayne Jackson, for graciously allowing me to use freely in the preparation of this manuscript materials he has authored on the inspiration of the Bible.]